# ON INSTINCTS

DIALECTIC AND SOCIETY

Lawrence Krader, Editor

*Board of Editors*

Agnes Heller, Budapest
Cyril Levitt (Assistant Editor), Hamilton, Canada
Angel Palerm, Mexico D. F.
Peter Stadler, Zürich

*Editorial Consultants:*

Y. S. Brenner, Utrecht
Alessandro Casiccia, Turin
Stanley Diamond, New York
Margrit Eichler, Toronto
Andre Fabregas, Mexico, D. F.
Ernest Gellner, London
Maurice Godelier, Paris
Manfred Hinz, Bremen
Marlis Krueger, Bremen
J. R. Llobera, London
Guido Martinotti, Milan

David McLellan, Kent
Claude Meillassoux, Paris
Ikenna Nzimiro, Nsukka
J. M. Ripalda, Madrid
Peter Skalnik, Leyden
Earl Smith, Connecticut
Jacob Taubes, Berlin
Charles B. Timmer, Amsterdam
Bianco Valota-Lavalotti, Milan
Bärbel Wallisch-Prinz, New York

1. Lawrence Krader, THE ASIATIC MODE OF PRODUCTION:
   Sources, Development and Critique in the Writings of Karl Marx

2. Lawrence Krader, DIALECTIC OF CIVIL SOCIETY

3. José Maria Ripalda, THE DIVIDED NATION
   The Roots of a Bourgeois Thinker: G. W. F. Hegel

4. George Márkus, MARXISM AND ANTHROPOLOGY
   The concept of 'human essence' in the philosophy of Marx

5. Lawrence Krader, A TREATISE OF SOCIAL LABOR

6. Agnes Heller, ON INSTINCTS

AGNES HELLER

# ON INSTINCTS

VAN GORCUM, ASSEN, THE NETHERLANDS   1979

ISBN 90 232 1705 5

Translated into English by Dr. Mario Fenyö
from the original Hungarian publication: 'Az ösztönökröl', published by Gondolat, Budapest, 1978.

Printed in The Netherlands by Van Gorcum, Assen

# CONTENTS

# INTRODUCTION

The essay which follows is the first of a series I plan to write about what may be described as 'social anthropology', for want of a better term. I say 'for want of a better term' for two reasons. One reason is purely technical: social anthropology is the term by which one of the most prominent schools of ethnologists in the Anglo-American world describes itself. In this connection I merely wish to point out that I do not belong to this school (even though I may have learnt a great deal from it), and that I use the concept in a different sense. The other reason for the possible ambiguity is theoretical. Since man is essentially a social being, there cannot be any kind of anthropology other than social; for everything that is specifically human in man's biological makeup has evolved socially and is socially determined, even if the ever 'given' social environment seems to be a 'natural' circumstance. History is the true natural history of man, said Marx, and if we take history in the broad sense of the term, meaning to include the millions of years-long process of auto-domestication, which is characteristic of the human species alone, this statement is undoubtedly valid. Nevertheless, it is not simply a matter of pleonasm to speak of 'social anthropology'. The term indicates where I mean to place the emphasis in my examination of the 'essence' of man. It indicates that in my analysis it is not the process of man becoming human that is primary, although I cannot avoid that type of examination altogether, nor is it the biological structure of contemporary man, although I cannot formulate my thesis with scientific pretensions without touching upon this matter, but rather the potentials contained in the human species. I do not expect to find these potentials in an eventual modification of the biological makeup of man, since I reject on the ground of my value choice the utopias (negative, in my opinion) aimed at the transformation of the genetical code, I reject the conceptions regarding some further 'mutation' of the species which have become current of late. According to my concept, we must seek the human potentials in the transformation of the second nature (the psychological-social nature), and not in that of his 'first nature'.

Allow me to quote Kuo's pertinent lines: 'In behaviour nature is what can be built in and not what is supposed to unfold from within... (of course, 'nature' can be built in only within the potential limit of the organistic pattern.).. .'[1]

Kuo's formulation is particularly pertinent, because he speaks of nature as manifested in behaviour, and not of 'nature' in general. For the 'organistic patterns' impose clear limits on 'building in'. To mention the most trivial of these: death is always the natural foreclosing of the potentials of the individual, an immortal humanity cannot be scientifically conceived. Or: man is able to prolong, as a consequence of compulsion, but also of self-will, the satisfaction of his biological needs (varying needs to a different extent), the fakirs may even consciously influence their 'caloric household' and their breathing, but there are some outer limits to this ability, not to mention that the extension of limits may not always be desirable everywhere. I could refer to less trivial and very current problems, for instance to the consequences of the disturbance of the ecological equilibrium, of the pollution of the environment, of the demographic increase which jeopardize the biological future of the species, to factors, in which taking account of the human organism's capacity of endurability becomes a social task and a norm. And what newer 'limits' one may encounter in this regard, we simply cannot know in advance. As far as behaviour is concerned, or, more precisely, the relationship of man to man, or the psycho-social structure of man, here there exists an infinite possibility for 'building in', in my opinion as well.

'Unfolding from within' and 'building in' are not mutually exclusive contradictions. Inasmuch as humanity can only realize its own potentials we have the right to say that it 'unfolds' these potentials. At the same time, however – and this is most important – something-that-does-not-yet-exist is born with every new type of activity, every new objectivation, value, or affect; and insofar as it does not perish, does not fall into oblivion, it will leave a trace in man's 'second nature' (his psycho-social nature), it becomes entrenched, it becomes the basis for further acts of 'building in', either in its positive or in its negative sense. When we say that humanity creates itself, and creates itself anew on the basis of that which is already created, we are actually speaking of the constant process of 'building in'.

The pushing back of the frontiers of nature and the 'building-in' of human nature are correlative even if not parallel processes in the individual, in every respect. At the level of the 'species-objectivations-in-themselves' (ansichseiende gattungsmässige Objektivationen) this correlation is clear. For instance nature constitutes an organic unity with the fixation of movement coordinations which create these tools and objects, or which are led by them, and with the building-in of the so created new

---

[1] Zing Yang Kuo, 'The Genesis of the Cat's Response to the Rat', in *Instinct*, ed. Birney-Teevan, Princeton: D. Van Nostrand, 1961, 25.

biological and psychological aptitudes into the nature of man. The conquest of external nature, or the building in of human nature into the individual can become independent only at the level of the 'species objectivations for themselves' (fürsichseiende gattungsmässige Objektivationen) even if only relatively. Thus law, morality, or art proposes (and already consciously at that) the building in of the 'second, the human nature', whereas the natural sciences, and only in the past few centuries, aim at the forcing back of the frontiers of external nature, but not without repercussions on the 'building-in' of human nature, of course.

I have said that the human organism, from the point of view of behaviour, is excessively malleable with regard to building in the 'second nature'. This notion, which in its present form is merely an unsubstantiated assertion, will become the subject of all those studies I shall devote to social anthropology (by now without quotation marks).

With this assertion, as I know full well, I have joined the minority of the thinkers of past and present. The majority of the philosophers, basing themselves not on biology and psychology, but on the experiences of their age, have argued that human nature resists 'building-in'. The theory of asocial desires and impulses which can only be guided or controlled by the mind, but can never cease, formulated already in Plato's *Phaedros*, is reborn under a variety of forms in bourgeois philosophy, in the oft expressed affect-reason dichotomy (in particular in modern psychology with the rigid separation of the cognitive and the emotional spheres). Man who is a wolf to man, unless checked by institutions and morality, or unless his wolfish nature finds channels of release, is a line of thought which goes from Hobbes to the theories of agression discussed in this treatise (even if today's ethologists-anthropologists have a better opinion of the wolf). And according to the predominant and thoroughly modern argument, the successful human building-in of the external nature leaves the internal nature untouched at best, or makes it even more asocial and irrational at worst, releasing instincts it has inherited from its animal ancestors. That civilization, the evolution of production leads to the building in of the 'bad' into an originally 'good' human nature – the idea presented by Rousseau – while it differs from the aforementioned thought in its conception of man, leads nevertheless to similar end-results.

While I do not believe that the process of mastering 'external nature' is anywhere nearly as advanced as the proponents of the myth of technology claim, and while I do not survey the status quo of internal nature with the pessimism of those I mentioned above, I cannot pretend that we are dealing with unfounded arguments. These arguments are based on quantities of data, and we must confront them. The beautiful and plastic idea according to which all we need is for man to develop his essential forces, and all he needs for this purpose is to bring about a human society which will make this possible for everyone, is something I myself accept, with one qualification: that 'all he needs' is indeed everything. It is present man who forms future society and the future men of present society. Can the human beings of the present, as they are today, form a society to the measure of the human beings of the future? And society, as it exists today, can it form a humanity to the measure of the society of the future? This is a 'chicken or the egg' problem, if you like, and if that's what it is, better to lay down the pen rather than waste my time in attempting to solve it. But if it isn't a 'chicken or the egg' problem, and I believe it isn't, then I must justify my faith (or confidence) in some way. And I must justify it without denying the facts of the present, and by examining all those question-marks many have placed next to the potential of man's 'second nature' becoming different from what it now is. It is the task of this essay, and of the subsequent ones, to question these questions-marks.

The themes of the six consecutive essays are 1) the instincts, 2) the theory of feelings, 3) the theory of needs, 4) the theory of morality, 5) the theory of personality and 6) the theory of history. Since these essays depend on each other in line of thought, I cannot indicate in advance in any one of them the attempts to solve the problem which will become the topic of the following works.

# I WHAT IS CALLED 'INSTINCT'?

The concept of instinct is one of the most ideological concepts science ever operated with. The very same empirical and experimental facts have given rise to the most diverse theories of instinct.

If we want to group the variety of theories of instinct we must begin first of all by asking whether they admit the existence of instincts at all. Thus the classical behaviourists deny the existence of instincts both in man and in animals. According to them all behaviour is learnt; the types of reaction born with individuals derive from experience during prenatal existence, thus for instance the 'pecking behaviour'. Other, less extreme behaviourists consider inquiries about the existence of instincts epistemologically irrelevant. We cannot gain any knowledge about instincts, concepts re instincts are 'abstract conceptions created to unify and make intelligible the observable behaviourial acts from which they are abstracted'.[2]

In the second category I group those who attribute the most varied instincts to animal and men alike. L. Bernard had tentatively counted up those specific types of action, forms of behaviour, impulses, or motives described as instincts by the innumerable theories which have seen light in the year directly preceding the appearance of his work: these amounted to more than 6,000. According to my classification, in the third group we find those who have reduced this multiplicity of instincts to a few basic ones and these have been interpreted primarily as the keys to animal and human behaviour. The ideological nature of the theory of instincts, as we shall see, is obvious in their case. Finally, in a fourth group we find those who would assign various instincts to animal races, but deny their significance in the case of the human species, or speak merely of instinct remnants. Not every researcher's conception can necessarily be placed into one of these four groups, but the classification nevertheless indicates the main trends.

I have said that the ideological nature of the concept of instincts is most clearly apparent in the case of the theory of basic instincts. The selection of basic instincts is not only simply of anthropomorphical provenance, but is largely a function of the experiences of a given period, particularly its social

[2] H. J. Eysenck, *The Structure of Human Personality*, John Dickens: Northampton, 1970, 2.

experiences. Undoubtedly, every so-called basic instinct is a philosophical abstraction, and the source of this philosophical abstraction is the historical and ideological 'basic experience' of the ever given present. Bernard presents a very apt critique of this manner of thinking without analysing its ideological origins:

> Thus such terms as fighting, gregariousness, self-assertion, self-abasement, acquisition, play, imitation and the like are not single and definite behaviour patterns. They are class terms for hundreds and thousands of concrete behaviour mechanisms which are grouped together in action or in conceptual thinking because of their general similarity of function. There are almost numberless ways of fighting, playing, imitating, or of having gregarious contacts with one's fellows. Each one of these may be a unit behaviour pattern and therefore entitled to be called an instinct, if it is inherited. But the whole list of activities having a common conceptual or classificatory name never occur in action together, that is, they never function as a unit behaviour process, as would be necessary if they were true instincts. . . An instinct is a biological fact and it is a unit character, or it does not exist. It is structural. It is not possible to inherit an abstraction.[3]

In the selection of the basic instincts – of these abstractions – it is indeed the function that is dominant, and precisely the function which is experienced as a basic function of human behaviour by the thinker accomplishing the selection, by the thinker who extends its existence in the animal world, and then generalizes it. Very typical from this point of view is the fate of the 'instinct of self-preservation' or even the fate of the 'social instinct'. The concept of 'instinct of self-preservation' has played a significant role in the 19th century, until the First World War, one might say. Today almost everyone speaks of the 'instinct of self-preservation' ironically. For how would it be possible to declare such radically different attitudes like escaping or hunting as one instinct? But other advocates of the theory of instincts speak with the greatest conviction of the 'play instinct' (again: how would it be possible to classify in the same group the process of learning, with the games pertaining to reproductive behaviour); or, as I shall analyse in detail, of the 'instinct of agression' where the fight amongst members of the same species during mating becomes the function of the same instinct as the fight between different species of rats. There can be no doubt, the instinct of self-preservation was considered a basic instinct at a time when the dominant historical experience was economic competition, when hunger was the main problem even in the

[3] Luther, L. Bernard, The Misuse of the Concept of Instinct in *Instinct*, Birney-Teevan (ed.), D. Van Nostrand Company, Princeton, Toronto, London, 1961, pp. 16-17.

'First World'. The economic struggle of self-preservation of everyone against everyone – this was the experience which determined the domination of the 'instinct of self-preservation'.

Naturally, the contemporary socialists could not accept it as the only basic instinct. Thus there appeared, as a sort of rival, the abstraction of 'social instinct', only to become, for Kropotkin and others, the leading instinct.[4]

For the same reason the theory of the 'instinct of aggression' has developed precisely in the 20th century, as a result of the experiences of the First World War, and became the dominating basic instinct in the theory of instincts, as a result of Fascism and the horrors of World War II. Since I will deal in detail with the theory of the instinct of aggression and its refutation further on, let us be satisfied, by way of illustrating the turn of fortune of instincts, with a brief analysis of the changes of the Freudian theory of instincts.

Freud, as is well known, evolved his theory of instincts in the aftermath of the First World War. Earlier he had talked about two basic instincts: the libido, and the 'ego instinct' or instinct of self-preservation. After the war he still maintained two basic instincts, Eros and Tanatos, that is the libido and the death instinct, the instinct of aggression or of destruction.

Proof of his scientific honesty and his genius is what Freud himself never denied: these can only be theoretical hypotheses, which function, in science, only as working hypotheses. At the time of the formulation of his first theory of instincts he wrote:

> I have proposed that two groups of such primal instincts should be distinguished: the ego, or self-preservating instincts, and the sexual instincts. But this supposition has not the status of a necessary postulate. . it is merely a working hypothesis, to be retained only so long as it proves useful, and it will make little difference to the results of our work of description and classification if it is replaced by another.[5]

And:

> The theory of the instincts is so to say our mythology. Instincts are mythical entities, magnificent in their indefiniteness. In our work, we cannot for a moment disregard them, yet we are never sure that we are seeing them clearly.[6]

---

[4] Well before the appearance of the concept of instincts one encounters these two distinct interpretations of the sources of human behavior. The former in Hobbes, for instance, the latter in Grotius.

[5] J. Freud: Instincts and their vicissitudes, in: Lindsay Hall: *Theories of Personality*, John Wiley and Sons, New York, London, Sydney, 1965, p. 6.

[6] *The Standard Edition of the Complete Psychological Works of Sigmund Freud*, Vol. XXII, 95pp, London, The Hogarth Press, 1964.

There can be no doubt, therefore, that both of Freud's pairs of instincts is the formulation of a life experience. Both pairs of instinct gave Freud the opportunity to describe scientific observations and experiences but, of course, they cannot be considered as scientifically verified in themselves. The motive of the selection of the instinct pairs is a life experience projected into philosophical mythology, the formulation of an ideological explanation of the world, or its reformulation.

But when I said that the various theories of the great basic instincts are the *most* obviously ideological, I did not mean to deny the more or less ideological roots of *every* theory of the instincts. For instance, C. Rogers refers to the theory of instincts of behaviourism based on exact experiments conducted in the laboratory or rather, their theory of the denial of instincts as 'sterile pseudo-science', analysing its connection with the philosophy of logical positivism. The description of behaviour as stimulus response expresses the technological world-view so obviously, and is so clearly the ideology of manipulation, that some of its representatives even consciously accept this connection, as a response to the criticism raised.

Until now I have discussed the main tendencies that can be distinguished in current theories, or in the theories that have had an impact unto this day, from the point of view of the existence or denial of the instincts. But I must make distinctions within the context of the question, and the narrower question would sound as follows: what do the representatives of the various theories of instincts consider specifically as instincts? Let it suffice to refer to the more than 6,000 instincts counted by Bernard in order to realise that here we are bound to speak only of main tendencies, even more so than before, and we cannot avoid oversimplifications.

Before broaching the critique of the theory of instincts I must give my own definition. Thus by instinct I mean those compulsory behaviour mechanisms or movement coordinations which are species-specific and at the same time action-specific, are inherited through the genetic code, elicited by internal and external stimuli, which play a leading role in the preservation of the species within a certain stage of the development of the living organism and which surpass the intelligence of the given species from the point of view of this positive selective value. I will attempt to justify this assumption below.

A common factor in every theory of instincts, at least among those with which I am familiar, is: instinct is something having compulsive force. This much I will accept myself. Even here I am bound to make a qualification, namely that I cannot accept the obverse of the relationship (which many have accepted), according to which everything that is innate and has compulsive force must be instinct. For there are a good many forms of behavior born with us and compulsive that cannot be classified among the instincts. Such is the case, in man, of expressive behaviour.[7] It is well known that human mimicry is compulsive by nature (and specific of the entire species, not learned, but innate). Neither crying nor laughing, neither the mimicry of sympathy nor of attention can be described as instinct (which, in any case, are characteristic of humans only), even though these are not learned behavior. (Darwin described the mimicry of a girl born blind and deaf, a mimicry that was species-specific even though she had not the possibility to learn).

Except for the innate character and for the 'compulsoriness' the various theories describe or define the nature of instincts in various manners. I want to characterise these various concepts with the two extreme approaches, since all others are essentially various attempts to synthesise the two extreme positions. According to one, the instincts are drive, motive, energy, whereas according to the other, the instincts are chains of unconditioned reflexes.

1. The drive-motive-energy concept is characteristic in the first place of those who represent the ideological concept of instincts, the theory of the so-called 'basic instincts', and who, either consciously, as in the cases of Mc-Dougall or Freud, or unconsciously, as in the majority of cases, identify instincts with affects; either by assigning an affect to each of the instincts, or by deriving the affects from given instincts. The Lorenz of the late period – as I shall show later on – represents this view rather well when dealing with the four great 'drives' (Trieb): hunger, sexuality, aggression and fear.

Instinct, therefore, is a 'drive' which 'moves' us, human and animal alike. It is a biological 'necessity', which must be satisfied, in order to live, in the broader sense of the term: in order to preserve ourselves and our race in the struggle for existence.

Since the ideological preference of this theory is that the selfsame 'great instincts' move humans and animals alike, it seems rather natural that it should 'pick' instincts that are not species-specific. Every animal is hungry, and so is man, every animal must reproduce, and so does man. But before turning to the critique of the theory I cannot refrain from making an ironical observation. I have always wondered why the need to drink, to sleep, or to excrete does not figure among the 'basic instincts', as far as the representatives of the ideological concept of instincts are concerned – except for Freud. If I consider the preference of ideology, the answer is simple. Although thirst is just as much of a drive (since we are talking about drives) as hunger, and is no less compulsive, it cannot figure among the 'great' instincts, because the satisfaction of these needs does not

---

[7] Anyway, expressions are not usually considered instincts, at most some of them are regarded as instinct remnants.

require, or requires only exceptionally – at least nowadays – the struggle for life hence they lack interest. And although forms of sleep or of excreting, in the case of man, are very social, the satisfaction of these needs does not collide with the satisfaction of the needs of others, hence does not create affects, etc.

As far as I am concerned – as I shall explain later – I do not consider the so-called drives as instincts, but as inner stimuli (following Tinbergen) which, at a certain stage of animal evolution (but not with human beings) and together with outside stimuli, elicit an instinctive act. I must add, however, that the inner stimuli resulting in instinctive acts are too dif-ferentiated to be described by motives called 'drives'. Lorenz whom I consider one of the great observers of nature, in the same class as Darwin, not only used to know this, but even discovered it, for instance when in connection with some bird species he talked of the independence of the instinct of nest-building and the instinct of 'padding' the nest from one another. No one knew as clearly as he did that the production of hormones and the stimuli produced by the central nervous system at their starting point are only exceptionally instinct-specific.[8]

The general theories of drive-instinct-energy, as I have said, consider the instinct thus understood as the general motive of behaviour or action. Of course, this line of thought appeals by its very simplicity inasmuch as every activity and behaviour can be directly or indirectly derived from two or more (but always from a few) basic compulsive motives. Of course, the deduction is always successful because, in the last analysis, everything can be derived from everything. Thus not only liking and loving can be derived from the libido but all kinds of creative activity, objectivation, etc. and from the social instinct (because it too is included on the list of drives), one can derive family and group solidarity, friendship, faithfulness, and even war (in the case of those who do not derive war from the 'instinct of aggression'). But the success of the deduction is far from proving an actual relationship. This type of deduction has rather ancient traditions, and reaches back to times when the concept of instinct was as yet unkown. Thus, for instance, the philosophy of the Enlightenment derived all human activity and institutions from *egoism* – with similar success.

As far as the concept of motives is concerned: although there is no space for analysis here, it may be ventured that, in my opinion, only specific motives exist, and only human beings have motives.

We have seen that the advocates of the drive theory identify all instincts with basic affects or, at least, ascribe basic affects to the basic instincts. At

---

[8] I am not speaking, in this context, about those who do not identify the concept 'drive' with the concept 'instinct'. Tension reduction, as the concept of drive reduction is compatible with various notions of instincts, and plays a role in behaviourist psychology which denies the existence of instincts. Many (thus Spiro) also apply it to the description of cognitive tasks.

the root of this concept there lies a basically false theory of affects, even if the representatives of the theory do not have an explicit theory of affects. According to this theory the affect is the opposite of *ratio* – and what is not rational (i.e. what is not based on insight, learning, or intellectual activity) is affective. The instinct, according to Arnold, 'diminishes consciousness', the affect also 'diminished consciousness', therefore the instinct is affective. Heinroth had said 'Animals are emotional people of extremely poor intelligence'.[9]

Since the analysis of affects is the subject of a subsequent essay, I would add only a few objections. It is undoubtedly true that the execution of instinctive acts presumes a certain 'state of excitation', but even in the case of animals the state of excitation is connected not merely to the execution of instinctive acts. Köhler's ape went into a fit or rage when he was unable to solve a problem, and it was with the appearance of the 'aha! experience' that his fit came to an end. But if we speak of human beings, then we must observe (and the experiments of Piaget, Vigotski, and my own personal experience authorise me to say so), that the solution of intellectual tasks is the source of greater 'excitation' and 'tension' even in the case of a three-year old than feeding – unless society does not guarantee him sufficient quantity of food which, unfortunately, is by no means a rare occurrence, but is not species-specific.[10]

Furthermore: to speak of affect in the case of animals is as much anthropomorphic as to speak of 'ratio' or, in other words, these concepts acquire partial meaning only where it is a matter of the 'instinct demolition', rather than the functioning of the instincts. But if we are making anthropomophic statements, then we may call the instincts, when they do exist, 'rational' with as much justification as 'affective'. Since security of instincts bears a positive selective value it is rational in the sense that it is purposive without purpose – in the Kantian sense of the concept.

It should be clear by now that I reject the identification of instinct-drive-motivation-energy not only in the case of human beings, but also with animals. Still, allow me to mention Gehlen's magnificent analyses to the effect that in man – for he only talks of man – the purely biological stimulus functions always as a social stimulus and need, deriving from man's nature oriented towards teleological action. Human *Antrieb* (stimulation – as Gehlen refers to the inner stimulus) includes not only satisfaction, but a tendency towards goal-oriented, i.e. socially defined kind

---

[9] Quoted by Konrad Lorenz, *Studies in Animal and In Human Behaviour,* Methuen and Co. Ltd., London, 1970, Vol. I, p. 251.

[10] Although, as I have already stated, it is possible to deduct everything. I may consider intellectual problem-solving, if I wish, a transposed expression of the libido. I may also do as Eibl-Eibesfeld had done, and speak of the 'instinct of learning' as a drive that is characteristic only of humans. But what good would it do?

of satisfaction. The circumstances of satisfaction play a major role in the realisation of purposiveness: the civilised hungry man does not lick up the food rejects from the floor. And here it is not at all a matter of conscious self-control, but of something elemental, disgust. Indeed, it is the function of conscious control that the starving man at the concentration camp does not steal the bread of his fellowman (and since it is only a matter of conscious control, it often happened that he did steal it,) but it is not the function of the conscious control that man cannot feed himself under circumstances that disgust him, and cannot satisfy his her sexual desire with a person towards whom he like feels (physical) repulsion. Hence we cannot speak of some new kind of 'counter-instinct' as in the case of the wolf, which does not eat the meat of conspecifics even when starving, because the social manifestations of human instinct are not 'species-specific', but vary according to culture.

2. I shall mention only briefly the concept opposite to the drive-energy instinct theory, because it has practically no followers today, at least no one of importance. According to them as I have said, instinct is the chain of unconditioned reflexes, rigid coordinations of movement that are elicited by specific outside stimulation. (See Ziegler, and Lorenz during the first period of his work). If I accepted this definition then, in the light of present observations and experiement, it is only in the case of insects that I could talk of acts of instinct, whereas the advocates of this theory ascribe instincts even to the vertebrates, and even to mammals – some even to man.

What are the main critical objections which render the above theory obsolete?[11]

First of all, that the selective behaviour oriented at the objects of instinctive acts are mostly learnt, an instinct-specific outer stimulus does not exist in every context and in every animal. It was an enormous accomplishment of Lorenz to demonstrate this by his discovery of imprinting (certain birds and, as it turned out, certain mammals as well, react to living objects they first perceive at a specific, early stage of development as to 'mother' or 'sibling': such objects may even be human.)[12] Furthermore: movement coordinations related to instinctive acts are not rigid, but modify according to the specific nature of the given object (they cannot be rigid, if only because orientation in space is also learnt, at least in case of the vertebrates). The examples could be multiplied.

The greatest problem with the advocates of 'the reflex chain theory', is that they only spoke of outer stimuli, and did not take into account the

---

[11] Those theories of reflex which recognise the role of inner stimuli are 'transitional' conceptions and I shall not mention them here.

[12] K. Lorenz, *King Solomon's Ring*, Methuen, London, 1952.

existence of inner stimuli as eliciting instincts. Craig, Tinbergen, and Lorenz have proved with whole series of observations and experiments that the so-called 'appetitive behaviour' is part of the instinctive act, that the animal does not relate to the outer stimuli, even in case of instinctive acts, in a passive manner, but in an active one, that he 'seeks out' the outer stimuli which elicit instinctive acts. The excellent observation of Lorenz about the possible 'vacuum activity' of the instinctive act is decisive in this context. Thus in case outer stimuli are omitted the instinctive act may be set off merely upon the influence of inner stimuli (that is, not at all as reflex), even without the presence of a 'substitute object'. (The bird which catches flies that do not exist, executes coordinated movement of catching and consuming the fly in the 'vacuum').

Since it is precisely in the case of man that the instinct remnants have sunk to the level of simple unconditioned reflexes – such as perhaps chewing, swallowing, and the frictional movement[13] – I can state without hesitation that the theory of unconditioned reflex-instinct is at least as anthropomorphic as the drive-motive theory.

Before attempting to analyse what I call instinct, and why, I would like to say a few words about those ethologists and anthropologists who have provided the scientific materials of my own concepts. They are: Craig, Lorenz (in his second period)[14] Tinbergen, Gehlen, and Claessens. The grounds of my choice – from a philosophical point of view – will be discussed at length later on. The ethologists have been my source primarily in the definition of animal instinct, whereas the anthropologists have been my source in connection with the analysis of human instinct demolition.[15] I must add, that it is not I who has established the connection between the aformentioned ethologists and anthropologists. These authors themselves refer to and build upon one another.

The trait they have in common is that they attempt to create a

---

[13] The examples are taken from Gehlen.

[14] In the first period of his development, Lorenz was an adept of the theory of the chain of unconditioned reflexes. Later, primarily as a result of his analysis of the experiments of Holst and of the reevaluation of his own experiences, he worked out the concept analysed here. In his last period, under the influence of Freudianism, he converted essentially to the concept of drive-instinct. I will criticise this last period of his thinking in detail later on, in connection with the theory of the instinct of agression. In the case of Gehlen I refer primarily to the notions expounded in *Der Mensch*. The 'right-wing radicalism' of Gehlen's sociology – to use the expression of Habermas – has left traces on his anthropology as well. Thus, in his ethics, and in opposition to the notions he himself had held earlier, he biologises human normative and social behavior. I have nothing to do with these views, as I do not have anything to do with Lorenz' later work.

[15] Of course, I do not have the opportunity to make a more detailed analysis of the aformentioned theories. I refer the reader to the following works: K. Lorenz, *Studies in Human and Animal Behaviour*; N. Tinbergen, *The Study of Instinct*; A. Gehlen, *Der Mensch* and Claessens, *Instinct, Psyche, Geltung*, Köln: Westdeutscher Verlag, 1968.

meaningful synthesis between the two extreme concepts of instinct, a synthesis which can be used to describe adequately the empirical experiences and the experimental facts. It is also their common trait that their concept of instinct precludes the possibility of ascribing instincts to man, or at least of ascribing instincts a decisive role in human behaviour and action. As Lorenz writes: 'Without a trace of doubt, human beings exhibit the *smallest* range of endogenous-automatic motor patterns found in any higher organism. Apart from certain motor norms of food-uptake (seizing, placing-in-the-mouth, chewing and swallowing), mating (frictional movements) and possibly certain automatic elements in walking and running, an adult human being appears to have no centrally coordinated motor patterns, based on endogenous automatisms'.[16] And according to Gehlen one of the main characteristics of human beings is 'the absence of genuine instincts, that is innate forms of movements reacting to certain eliciting schemata'.[17]

According to this interpretation, therefore, instinct is defined as movement coordination given by the genetical code, that is, born with every member of the species. The principle of movement coordination excludes both the theory of 'basic instincts' and the 'theory of drives'. If instinct is movement coordination then it is impossible, for reasons of principle, to speak of basic instincts, unless anthropocentrically. 'Reproductive behaviour' (an expression consciously and fittingly used in lieu of the 'sexual instinct') is a sequence of a great many, various, and separate movement coordinations (that is, instincts), what more, of movement coordinations that differ according to the species. Thus for instance, 'imposing behaviour' is the precondition of reproduction in some species, albeit in different ways, whereas it is totally lacking in others. But just as there is no 'sexual instinct' or 'social instinct', there is likewise no 'parental instinct', no basic instinct whatever which would motivate or regulate the specific instincts. 'In my opinion, the fact that the functional unity of a component functional system, supposedly governed by one 'parental instinct' can be disrupted by the absence of a minor morphological character is proof of the autonomy and equivalence of the individual behaviour patterns involved'.[18]

At the same time, however, as I have already mentioned, an organic part of the above definition of instincts is the appetitive behaviour, the inner stimulus that elicits instincts, that is, the activity of instincts. And what is very important from this point of view: the inner stimulus itself is not an instinct, no more than the outer stimulus, both being but the condition of

[16] K. Lorenz, *Studies in Animal and Human Behaviour*, op. cit.,
[17] Arnold Gehlen, 'Zur Systematik der Anthropologie' in *Studien zur Anthropologie und Soziologie* Luchterhand, Berlin/Neuwied, 1963, 35.
[18] K. Lorenz, *op. cit.,* I, p. 294.

species-specific instinctive acts. (The vacuum activity does not contradict this assumption: if the vacuum activity were species-specific, the instinct would lose its function and be demolished). According to Tinbergen's description the movements carried out at the beginning of the 'exploratory behaviour' are as yet hardly stereotyped, they remain rather individual, and it is only as a result of 'complementary stimuli' that species-specific movement coordinations come about, if they do which is not always the case. The most rigid movement coordination − as Craig described it − is the so-called 'end reaction' (and it is from these that those instinct remnants − the existence of which no one seems to doubt − have come about in human beings: for instance, chewing, swallowing, suckling, the frictional movement). Thus the 'inner stimulus' is not an instinct in itself (instinct is not drive), but there can be no instinctive act without an inner stimulus.

Allow me to quote, by way of summing up the presentation, Tinbergen's definition of instinct; 'A consideration of the neurophysiological relationship underlying instinct leads to a definition of 'an instinct' in which the responsible nervous centres and their mutual inhibition are also taken into account ... I will tentatively define an instinct as a hierarchically organised nervous mechanism which is susceptible to certain priming, releasing and directing impulses of internal as well as of external origin, and which responds to these impulses by coordinated movements that contribute to the maintenance of the individual and the species.'[19]

Among the anthropologists it was Gehlen and Claessens who have drawn the consequences from an essentially similar definition of instincts with regard to human beings. The formation of man is the history of the instinct demolition and not of the demolition of particular instincts − this occurs frequently in the animal world as well − but the general history of the demolition of instinct guidance. According to Gehlen the two main characteristics of man are: his being unspecialised (*unspezialisiertes Wesen*), and the so-called *hiatus*. Not being specialised means precisely the demolition of specific movement coordinations (i.e. instincts). Man as a teleological being is capable of an infinite number of typical movement coordinations. The openness of man consists precisely in his being capable of all kinds of movement coordinations, that is, it is identical with the statement that the overwhelming majority of movement coordinations are not species-specific. Hiatus, on the other hand, means that the movement coordinations and types of behaviour are not biologically given (again, they are not species-specific, but are cultural). Why is it hiatus? Because in the case of animals the inner stimulus − along with the outer stimulus of the environment − brings about the behaviour typical of the species in the

[19] N. Tinbergen, *The Study of Instinct*, Oxford, Clarendon Press, 1951, pp. 111-112.

biological organism itself. The inner stimulus subsists in humans as well (hormonal processes in the form of stimuli released by the central nervous system), but the action resulting from them is not biologically determined. First of all, man does not have an 'environment' (Umwelt) but a world (Welt), he is not confronted, or only exceptionally, with simple 'stimuli', but rather with social expectations, objects, customs, and norms. It follows from this that various types of behaviour, movement coordinations, etc., come into existence as a result of the appropriation of the social world. Claessens starts from this when he formulates the theory according to which it is not the inner 'stimulus' that takes over the role of the instincts (the inner stimulus is not instinct, according to him, even in animals), but the system of social customs and institutions. It is the system of customs and institutions that ensures in every culture although with differing contents the 'security' of action which is 'instinctive' in the case of animals: this is ensured by rigidity, repetition and repeatability, by regulation; last but not least, by the fact that the schemata of behaviour and movement coordination, basic from the point of view of the preservation of society, can be carried out without conscious pondering, 'instinctively' as it were, that is, by the so-called 'second nature'.

The system of species objectivations in itself (an-sich-seiende gattungsmässige Objektivationen)[20] parallel with the demolition of the biological system of instincts – to speak figuratively – takes over their role, and 'leads' the actions and behaviour of the individual in the reproduction of himself, his society, his species. Since this objectivation is always learnt, acquired, created and reconstitued in its specific contents, the most diverse systems of objectivation may fill this function. Yet, precisely because with humans there is no instinct guidance, human world and life is not possible without the system of 'species objectivations in itself'. Man is not a social animal, but a social being. As Lorenz writes: 'When young people are growing up, they are extensively moulded by the society in which they develop. When young jackdaws grow up they form a jackdaw society complete to the last detail with no prior image'.[21]

Before turning to the exposition of my own definition of instincts I must refer to what I had said about the ideological nature of theories of instincts. Few concepts in science are as permeated with ideology as the concept instinct. My choice of ethnologists and anthropologists as the scientific sources of my own concept of instincts was not prompted, and intentionally not prompted, simply by their description of empirical and experimental facts in a manner which was free of contradiction. In my choice, I was led – consciously, I must emphasise – by my philosophical

[20] S. my book, *Everyday Life*, forthcoming in English at Routledge and Kegan Paul.
[21] K. Lorenz, *op. cit.*, I, 255.

conception and values (these two being inseparable). I sought a concept of instincts which, on the one hand corresponds to the facts uncovered by the empirical and experimental science at its present level, but at the same time satisfies my philosophical, theoretical and my value hypotheses as well.

Yet, if the facts and their scientific interpretation had contradicted my values and philosophical hypotheses, I would have been obliged to modify at least the latter. But a careful examination of the materials and of the interpretations have led me to conclude that the facts not only could theoretically be interpreted along the line of my own theories and values, but that the strongest facts and the most convincing interpretations also suggest this interpretation. This was the only basis on which I could pretend – without attempting to hide my value preference and my philosophical hypotheses – to formulate my definition of instincts as the most probable scientific truth, and to judge other theories on this basis.

What were these theoretical hypotheses and value preferences? First of all I sought a concept of instincts on the basis of which I could argue for the 'openness', the 'plasticity' of man, on the basis of which we could accept as fact what I had mentioned in the Introduction: that from the point of view of behavior human nature is not identical with what 'unfolds from within', but what can be built in. I have sought a concept of instinct which would allow for the infinite potential of human nature; for the man of the future cannot be extrapolated from present man, or at least we are not obliged to extrapolate him. I have sought a concept of instinct which does not contradict the assumption that, in a chosen future, the world created by man, and man created by the world, will differ from today's world and today's man in certain constituents that are far from being of negligible importance.

This value – premise, however, is not *per se* a clear description of the character of the concept of instinct I had selected. This prospect of the future – a prospect I myself would opt for – can be assumed and constructed on the basis of the drive-motive-instinct theory as well. And many have actually assumed such a thing: thus Eibl-Eibesfeld, according to whom altruism is an innate instinct, and it is precisely this instinct that guarantees a future worthy of man. Or those followers of Freud who have retained the libido as sole drive-energy, a libido which will surely lead to a humanised state of society once certain frustrating social circumstances are eliminated. The theory of basic instincts is also appropriate for this purpose: suffice to mention the 'social instinct' of Kropotkin. And vice-versa: among those who deny the existence of instincts there are a number who consider such a view of the future as utopistic: thus, for instance, Dollard and his followers, whose theory of frustration-aggression I will endeavour to discuss later on.

The other philosophical hypothesis which has had a decisive influence on the selection of my interpretation of instincts has been Marx's idea of the essence of man.[22] According to Marx the constituents of the human species essence are: sociality, consciousness, objectivation, universality, and freedom. These are what characterise humanity since its formation, as opposed to the world of animals, hence these are the potentials of man. The process of realisation of these potentials is human history itself. 'The human species essence' develops in the objectivations that come about in the historical process, but in an alienated form; the gap between the potentials of the development of the individual, and the development of the species becomes ever wider. It is only in the present age (I mean the age of Marx himself and the immediate aftermath) that those economic conditions which would permit man to overcome alienation, which would make it possible for the individual to acquire and realise the wealth of the species, have actually come about.

The second part of the train of thought would indicate clearly why the notion of 'building-in' versus 'unfolding from within' is so important to me. The potentials of the species in the form of capacities may develop as a result of the social division of labour without being built in the individuals, and without even becoming capable of this building-in. The possibility of appropriation of the species essence by every individual[23] – something which remains yet to be proved – is according to Marx and in my own opinion 'real history', and thus becomes absolutely necessary for the further development and building-in of the capacities of the species, in a process that is intended by and conscious to, everyone.

Let us now survey the constituents of the Marxian 'species essence' in somewhat greater detail, and from the specific aspect of the questions raised in this treatise. I should add that these constitutents are all essentially related to one another, hence their independent analysis is not exempt from analytical abstraction.

1. The social is what is not the natural; the evolution of sociality signifies, by the same token, rolling back the boundaries imposed by nature, meaning the boundaries of both internal and external nature. This entails two consequences. On the one hand, the fact that it is specific of human species: in other words, that the 'species essence' cannot be derived from the biological and natural circumstances. On the other hand, that this same 'species essence' cannot be isolated from those natural

[22] Regarding the line of thought of Marx see Markus, *Marxizmus és 'antropologia'* Marxism and 'anthropology' (Van Gorcum, Amsterdam). I have attempted to show in my essay titled 'Hypothesis regarding a Marxist theory of values', that Marx's theory about the constituents of the essence of the species itself is based on a choice of values.

[23] This appropriation, as I have explained in detail in my work, *Everyday Life,* does not signify that every individual realises every potential of the species, but rather than he may realise any of these potentials. Furthermore, he may develop a conscious relationship to his species character.

circumstances which have allowed it to come about, and in the rolling back of which it is constituted anew and anew. The first philosophical assumption contradicts the theory of drive-instincts as characteristic of man and animal alike and which would essentially motivate both. And from the second assertion it follows that it is the unceasing 'task' of man as social being to satisfy his biological needs as communicated socially. This is why I consider the extreme behaviourist position untenable; for instance that of A.F.C. Wallace, according to whom neither breathing, nor eating, sleeping, play, parental activity, hunting, fear, nor even sexuality are essential features of man as cultural being: the essence of man is to be found exclusively in the ability to solve cognitive problems which can be abstracted from the biological.

2. The notion of consciousness includes several aspects, albeit inter-related. First of all the fact that within the trinity: instinct-conditoned action-intelligence, it is intelligence that assumes the leading role in man; even in the majority of drilled acts the starting point is (intellectual) recognition. Man is a teleological being who realises set objectives and selects the appropriate means for their realisation. Lingual thinking which enables him to formulate and transmit informations beyond perception belongs to the essence of man; thus he can transcend his environment. His intelligence renders superfluous instinct as mechanism of adaptation. For one thing, within the rather elastic limits ensuring the homeostasy of the organism, he can adapt to anything, for another thing the adaptation is but a subordinate aspect of his activity; increasingly he uses nature itself for the satisfaction of his varying needs.

3. Man becomes objectified in the products of his own work, in his institutions and systems of customs, in his language, his principles and values, his *Weltanschauungen* and his arts. The world he creates is, indeed, created and recreated by particular persons, yet it has an existence relatively autonomous from those persons. The world is an object for the individual, only man is subject. 'Man makes his life activity itself into an object of will and consciousness'.[24] This quoted thought will play a rather significant role in my further arguments. The fact that human being is the only being characterised by 'ambiguity', that is, he is an ego who is able to know and to shape the ego from the point of view of someone else (and only because of this can be considered ego), that is to say, the fact that man has self-knowledge and self-consciousness (he exists as a conscious ego and frequently enjoys consciousness of the ego), is the main condition and creative aspect of his 'plasticity'.

'Passion is man's essential capacity energetically bent on its object', says

[24] Karl Marx, *From Excerpt-Notes of 1844*, in: Writings of the Young Marx on Philosophy and Society (Lloyd, D. Easton and Kurt H. Guddat, translators and editors) Anchor Books, Doubleday. New York, 1967, p. 294.

Marx.[25] What is now most important to us, from our point of view, is the object-orientedness of the affect. We can understand the affect (and the motive as well) only within the context of the relationship between subject and object; and this is yet another argument against the theory of drive-motive-instinct. Since the theory of feelings will be the subject of a subsequent treatise, let me stick to the subject of the theory of instinct in its narrower sense, and let me analyse briefly the so-called sexual instinct.

To briefly summarise what I had already said about the matter above: if the instinct is species-specific movement coordination and innate then there can be no sexual instinct as such, the term 'reproductive behaviour' groups under a single concept the most varied instincts from the point of view of function and failing which – if we consider the matter from a functional point of view – fertilisation may still take place without the slightest hitch. Man's only remnant of instinct that has something to do with sex is frictional movement – but this does not exist in the case of unnumerable vertebrates, not to speak of insects! Animals do not have a sexual attitude at all, if only because their sex hormones are periodically produced and, with the exception of the periods of reproduction, – under natural circumstances as regards the evolution of the species – reproductive behaviour simply does not occur.

Sexual behaviour is not 'sexual instinct', but was very much born with mankind. Sexual behaviour exists only when sexual desire finds an object (that is, beginning with the formation of the subject-object relationship), when periodicity ceases, where sexual desire and sexual relationship create rapports independently from the creation of heirs or their education. (Since man has consciousness, it is most decisive in his case that there is a connection between sexuality and the birth of heirs). The birth of sexuality is contemporaneous with the birth of the incest taboo, that is, with a social, rather than instinctive regulation.[26]

4. I have already analysed an important aspect of universality by quoting Gehlen, according to whom man is the only non-specialised being. When Marx claims that man produces not only according to the rules of his own species, but according to the rules of every species, he is actually sketching the consequences of the instinct demolition, from the point of view of universality. (There is no point in wasting words on the fact that whatever happens according to the rules of only one's own species is not yet production). The reference concluded the line of thought, up to the 'production according to the measure of beauty' which actually refers to a

---

[25] *Id.*, p. 327.
[26] Lorenz, before assuming the arguments of the neo-Freudians, often makes fun of those who describe as 'animal' something that can be found only in man or, at best, among the over-domesticated animals.

deeper aspect of universality: to the creation of spheres of objectivation – what more, structured and regulated spheres – which no longer have anything to do with the satisfaction of biological needs, even socially transmitted.

Since man is a universal being, his capacities become needs at the same time (and, vice-versa, his needs become capacities). Since I will discuss the relationship of this problem in my theory of needs further on, I will now mention only some aspects relevant to my present argument. First of all, that knowledge itself becomes a need in man. The more man becomes universal, the more intensively and extensively infinite the potentials of knowledge, the less the so-called reduction exists from precisely the point of view of this basic and human drive. The need for knowledge is, of course, but an example of the groups of needs that are independent of biological stimuli, and the common feature of which is the sustaining of the state of tension or, rather, its perennial renewal independently from biological factors. I have already stated elsewhere: the alienated and strictly human need, the desire of possession, likewise cannot be reduced (of course, only as long as it exists and as long as alienation exists). The desire for possession is precisely the alienation of universality in its form of secondary specialisation. The compulsive motives that are not characteristic of mankind today (of civilised mankind) are, for the most part, such secondary drives, which certainly do not have an animal origin, but are values or non-values created by human universality, hence cannot be satiated as can the primary drives. (For instance, if my love returns my love, this is not 'drive reduction', but fulfillment).

Another word about the need for universality.[27] The need for the manifold development of the capacities of the individual can only come about where and when the objectivations leading it already exist, or can be imagined, postulated; and under forms in which they are present or can be assumed. It is only in this sense that I may talk here of a species-specific need, or drive. There can be no desire without object (even if it be merely an ideal object), and there is no ability without activity.

5. Freedom – looking at it only from the point of view of this treatise – means first of all an openness to the future, the possibility of consciously and intentionally realising the new, that which has not yet been. Thus the freedom of man – as opposed to the condition of the animal – is first of all self-creation: beginning, as an abstract potential in the process of self-domestication, continuing in 'prehistory' (we ourselves create it, but under conditions alien from us, under conditions 'already given'), and finding completion in the 'real history', in which the 'inherent measure' of human species is applied to history as well.

---

[27] This need plays a prominent role in the theories of the so-called 'third trend' of American psychology. I shall return later on to an analysis of this school.

Everything I have said about the four preceding constituents of the 'species essence' is also an aspect of human freedom. Still – and this is relevant from the point of view of the subject of this treatise – I must make a differentiation. In the case of the four preceding constituents it is possible that they be achieved on the level of the species – in 'species objectivations' (gattungsmässige Objektivationen) without being appropriated by the individuals of the society. Universality is possible, on the level of the 'species objectivations', along the one-sided specialisation of the individuals; the boundaries of the external nature may be rolled back, and the conquest of societality in the external nature may be infinite without 'inner nature' being 'built-in' the individual – except for the movement coordination. The greatest degree of consciousness is possible in the direction of society – although there has been no example of this, albeit such a utopia may be posited since the discovery of the genetic code – even along with the artificial corruption of the consciousness of masses of individual human beings; objectivation remains possible in spite of the disuse of the capacities appropriate for objectivation. But freedom is not possible, never possible without the freedom of the individuals. Knowledge, and the evolution in the transformation of nature does not necessarily entail the growth and realisation of freedom, in which the development of abilities and of self-control, as well as control over our own products become a unified process. As Goethe said: 'Everything which emancipates our spirit without ensuring power over ourselves, is destructive.'[28]

I have described above, however briefly, those theoretical and value assumptions which have played a part in the formation of my theory of instincts. Now let me repeat the contents of my interpretation of instincts: ... by instinct I mean those compulsory behaviour mechanisms or movement coordinations which are species-specific, and at the same time are action-specific, inherited through the genetic code, elicited by internal and external stimuli which play a leading role in the preservation of the species within a certain stage of the development of the organism and which surpass the intelligence of the given species from the point of view of this positive selective value'.

Briefly, about some aspects of this definition:

Instincts are 'inherited through the genetic code', hence the informations accumulated in them are purely biological, and do not derive for experience; they are not learnt.

Instincts are 'elicited by internal stimuli', that is to say, they are no chains of unconditional reflexes. These internal stimuli themselves are not 'species-specific' but metabolic processes, acts of hormone production,

---

[28] Goethe, J. W., *Sämtliche Werke*, Leipzig, Cottischer Verlag, 1863, I, 1243 – rough translation.

stimuli emitted by the central nervous system which can be character traits in common of species with diverse instinct guidance.

The instincts are 'elicited by external stimuli', the latter may or may not be species-specific. (Thus the most varied species of animals may react to the sound of a rifle shot, but always with a series of motion coordinations that are species-specific.) The stimulants themselves may be given in the genetic code (when the particular stimulus that will provoke a particular movement coordination is determined in the animal from birth), but they may also be learnt as the above example has shown (conditioned stimuli are those which elicit an instinctive act). The presence of an external stimulus is not always necessary to elicit an instinctive act in the case of a particular animal vacuum activity, but it is necessary if we consider the species.

Instincts are 'behaviour mechanism or movement coordinations' which are species-specific, that is, they are characteristic of every healthy specimen. They may modify or transform only by means of mutation, that is, in the process of development of a new species.

Instincts 'are behaviour mechanisms or movement coordinations which are action-specific' meaning that they always manifest themselves in the behaviour pertaining to a specific action, and cannot be reduced to their individual components. 'Reduction to their elements', or the separate or isolated provocation of movement coordinations always signify that we are dealing with different instincts. There are no general instincts such as social, sexual, escape, motherly, or aggressive instincts.

The instinctive act is compulsive; it takes place unconditionally as a result of the impact of internal or external stimuli at least in the case of healthy specimen.

The instincts 'play a leading role in the preservation of the species within a certain stage in the development of the organism'. Innumerable groups of invertebrates barely have instincts, the biochemical processes fill the function of positive selective value directly. Insects are the animals most clearly guided by instincts – and this may be the very reason why they constitute a dead-end from the point of view of evolution.[29] In the case of vertebrates the guidance of the instincts is increasingly 'combined' with behaviour learnt by means of 'trial and error' based on conditioned reflexes and, exceptionally in the case of certain species, it is combined with actions of insight guided by intelligence. In the latter case the animal finds the solution all at once, without trial and error. Thus the instinct demolition, for which man provides the only example, begins, as a process,

---

[29] Whether evolution itself is an anthropocentric concept which can only be understood from the aspect of 'development towards man', that is from the birth of mankind considered as positive value, or whether it is a concept of natural science free of any value – this is a far-reaching problem which I do not wish to discuss here.

already with the differentiation of the vertebrates. Nevertheless, even in the case of the higher order of mammals the instincts play at least as important a role in the preservation of the species as do the various types of learnt behaviour. The only exception is the domestic animal, and first of all the dog which, however, is no longer capable of survival in a natural environment, unless by regression.

'From the point of view of positive selective value the instincts surpass the intelligence of the species.' If a given species can solve a certain task by means of learning, its instincts in that respect will always be demolished. With the principal mammals more and more learned actions stop the acts of instincts, and the combination of acts of instincts and actions learnt becomes ever more frequent. Here I would like to reiterate the following: those behaviour and movement coordinations that have a compulsive force and are provided in the genetical code, and which have no positive selective values, do not play a role in the preservation of the species and of the individual, they are not instincts. Thus expressions are not instincts (the dog wags his tail or pulls it between his legs, points his ears, etc.) just as no kind of biological fact can be an instinct (the sense of smell, sight, hearing) which are species-specific, which do have a positive selective value, yet are not behavioural movement coordinations, but merely the conditions for these.

It was necessary to say all this in order to repeat, this time on better grounds: man is not an instinct-guided being, what more, human beings do not have instincts at all, only instinct remnants. These are limited to certain, very few movement coordinations which require a mimimum amount of intelligence; and as Darwin had already noted, even these are in the process of being demolished.

'On somewhat better grounds', I have reiterated what I had stated at the very beginning; but, of course, the grounds are far from good enough. To provide really solid grounds a detailed analysis of certain 'human instincts' called 'drives' will be necessary (because it is only the advocates of the theory of drives who continue to speak nowadays of human instincts). Let me refer once again to the 'calculations' of Bernard, to more than six thousand motivations, drives, or attitudes referred to as instinct. The detailed analysis, a well argued refutation obliges me to pick one out of this multitude of instincts; I have picked the so-called 'instinct of aggression', and not at all by chance.

Let us recall how in the 20th century the instinct of aggression has taken the place of the 'instinct of self-preservation', and how its analysis has become practically the key topic of every theory of drives and instincts in the aftermath of fascism and of the Second World War. And it should come as no surprise that aggression, as a psychological manifestation, is the principal topic in the camp of those who deny the existence of instincts as

well. Thus the analysis of 'aggression' is particularly suited for the exhaustive critique of the drive – instinct theory, as well as for the critique of the range of problems raised by the likewise ideological behaviourists and other tendencies.

Nevertheless, in picking the problem of aggression I was motivated primarily by my own preconceptions regarding the philosophy of history and my own choice of values. Neither the idea that aggressivity is innate as instinct, nor the notion that aggressivity is the necessary answer of an ego to the existence of objectivations, of the system of social norms, or of the hiatus, can be reconciled with what I have stated of the species essence, the 'plasticity' of human nature, the possibilities for 'building--in' capacities. At the same time I do not belong among those who, while not denying the existence of phenomena grouped under the term aggression, consider their elimination as a rather simple process based on 'insight', thus neglecting all those social and psychological factors which occur as obstacles between the desired future and the present situation.

I will elaborate my critical remarks in relation to the fundamental concepts of the various schools. First I will examine the theory of the instinct of aggression (the traditional type of naturalism), secondly behaviourism, neo-freudianism and environmentalism, thirdly the so-called 'third school' of American psychology (naturalism based on personality theory). Finally – in the fourth place – I will outline my own questions.

## II THE THEORIES OF THE INSTINCT OF AGGRESSION, OR TRADITIONAL NATURALISM

### 1. THE GENESIS

The 'instinct of aggression' (as well as the concept of aggression of environmentalism) is a bottomless bag into which it is possible to stuff the most diverse behaviours, attitudes, impulses, activity types, feelings, or character traits. Should someone commit parricide, slam the ink-bottle to the floor, play chess, work, be jealous or envious, take revenge, be angry, play football or watch the game, write a book, or should he entertain prejudices, should he argue, shoud he condemn or accuse, should he prohibit or act in disregard of prohibition, should he revolt or not revolt, whould he do business, make friends or love, or should he not make friends and not make love — all of this could be ascribed as a subtle or not so subtle manifestation of man's 'instinct (or drive, or motive) of aggression'. This curious homogenization is more or less typical of every theory of aggression, but particularly so of the idea of the instinct of aggression.[30] The contents of this peculiarly homogenized 'catch-phrase' are, naturally, 'divided' in two: into the compartments of the 'useful' and of the 'harmful' manifestations of the aggressive instinct. Consistent thinkers, such as Freud, assume the position that if the 'instinct of aggression' exists, none of its manifestations can be eliminated'.[31] Likeable, but theoretically far from consistent followers of Freud — such as Horney, Erikson, Fromm — have attempted, on the contrary, to solve the task that is basically insoluble on the basis of the given theory, namely the elaboration of a prospect according to which the 'useful' forms of aggression can be retained whereas the 'harmful' ones can be disposed of. But it is characteristic of every theory of the instinct of aggression, that the homogenization abstracts from everything that is socially and psychologically (the two being related but not identical) essential in an action, a character trait, etc.: thus from the situation, the function, the value, the

[30] The scheme according to which a behaviour, as well as its opposite can both be described by the term aggression was actually discovered by Freud when dealing with the so-called self-aggression or self-destruction. Thus, if I revolt, that is aggression, whereas if I don't revolt but submit, that is self-aggression.
[31] See his correspondence with Einstein in which he argues the impossibility of doing away with wars.

26

meaning and, last but not least, from its relation to the entire personality. My objection, therefore, is not that this homogenization is an abstraction, but rather that it is an abstraction without content, an abstraction that does not contribute to the knowledge and solution of the problems.

The theories regarding the genesis of the instinct of aggression may be roughly divided into two. According to one concept the aggressive instinct of man is rooted in his animal origins; one of the basic instincts of higher order animals being the 'instinct of aggression,' which also remains the basic instinct of the social animal (to use Aristotle's expression), of man. This is how Freud often, if not always, analyzes 'the instinct of death', this is how Mitcherlich analyzes his own 'destrudo', and it is this notion that guides Lorenz in his *On Aggression* of his late period. According to the other concept, the instinct of aggression is a peculiarly human drive, intra-specific aggression being exclusively characteristic, of all living beings, of man. The advocates of this interpretation find the causes of the formation of the instinct of aggression in man's particular natural history, in the history of the formation of mankind. Thus, according to them, aggression is precisely specific to the human species. These two main tendencies cannot be sharply differentiated from one another, and there are a number of transitional theories. Moreover, in the second interpretation, the use of the term 'instinct' is not quite clear. (There are some who tie the formation of aggression, as an irresistible drive characteristic of the entire human being, to the demolition of instincts, using two different concepts of instinct as applied to man and to animals). I will return to these variations when discussing the analysis of Eibl-Eibesfeld, Kluckhohn, Dart, and Kurth. Nevertheless, they share the thought – and this is what's important from our point of view at the moment – that in the case of 'aggression' we are dealing with a drive that is characteristic of the human species in general, of something given to the individual through the genetic code, of something having the force of compulsion.

For a critical description of the first tendency I have chosen the work of Lorenz. It is here that we can see most clearly how a concept of instinct is transformed in accordance with a new ideological preference – and not by just an ordinary scientist, but by one of the greatest ethologists of our time.

Let us first take a look at Lorenz' definition: 'The subject of this book is aggression, that is to say the fighting instinct in beast and man, which is directed against members of the same species'.[32]

Thus Lorenz already posits the existence of a separate instinct (general drive) in the case of animals, an instinct which motivates intraspecific fight. At the same time he classifies the instinct of aggression among the

---

[32]  Konrad Lorenz, *On Aggression*, Bantam Books, New York, Toronto, London, 1969, p. IX.

four basic instincts. These are, according to him, 'hunger, sexuality, aggression and fear'.[33]

These two thoughts tie together ideologically two assertions that are incompatible according to the laws of natural science, as Lorenz himself might have argued in his earlier theory. It is common knowledge, and no one knows it better than Lorenz himself, that intraspecific aggression, even if we consider only vertebrates, is characteristic of only some species. Furthermore, practically all those forms of behaviour he describes as 'instinct of aggression', pertain to the instinct of reproductive behaviour; hence, even if I do no make allowance for the use of the term 'sexual instinct', it nevertheless belongs to that group according to Lorenz' terminology. Tinbergen, in his book on the social behaviour of animals, demonstrates with regard to every form of intraspecific fight that it is an organic part of 'reproductive behaviour', except for the fight among certain species of birds for the sake of hierarchy in the so-called pecking order. The very first example analysed in the book of Lorenz — the territorial fight of the coral fish against intruders of their own species — clearly belongs within the realm of 'reproductive behaviour'. The only example cited by Lorenz I, as layman, do not see as related to reproductive behaviour, are the wars of extermination waged by colonies of rats against one another. But even if there were fifteen such examples, their number would still not justify classifying the 'instinct of aggression' among the 'four great' instincts (assuming it means only intra-specific fight).

The analysis of aggression as intra-specific fight follows from the anthropocentric features of the theory of Lorenz. Furthermore, it is an anthropocentrism that is derived particularly from the psyche of contemporary man. Of course, modern man is not enraged, when he twists the neck of the chicken, and he requires no internal stimulus to slaughter his pig. The combat, if it can be referred to as such, is most unequal. But we need no lively fantasy to imagine that in the early paleolithic, when hunting entailed mortal danger, things were rather different. (And this is where a number of representatives of the other theory of the instincts of aggression start from in their explanation of the genesis of aggression). Lorenz projects the psyche of modern man into the world of animals as well: 'The fight between predator and prey is not a fight in the real sense of the word. . . The inner motives of the hunter are basically different from those of the fighter'.[34] He infers these 'inner motives' in retrospect from the expressive movements. The expression of the dog who catches the rabbit is 'happy'. It is only the counter-attack against the animal of prey that 'better resembles' 'true' aggression. Yet what does it mean, to

---

[33] K. Lorenz, *op. cit.*, p. 211.
[34] Id., p. 23.

28

'resemble'? The expression of the rabbit, when caught by the dog, is surely not 'happy'. Whereas the life and death struggle of animals of relatively equal force, but of different species, can be characterized by the expression of 'rage' as much as the fight between members of the same species, if not more so: we hardly need be an ethologist to know this. Or let us mention the 'enraged expression' of the mother animal in case of any danger emanating from members of another species against her young ones. The former, the hunt, can be motivated, I suppose, by hunger. And the defence against the animal of prey? And the defence of the offspring? Because, according to Lorenz, by no means can it be motivated by aggression (defined by him as intra-specific fight). Then, perhaps by fear, it being one of the four basic instincts? We could argue this were it not for the fact that Lorenz defines the four basic instincts in several instances, but in varying ways: 'hunger, love, fight, flight',[35] or 'hunger, sexuality, flight, and aggression'.[36] But then fear cannot be either defence against the animal of prey, or the drive of defending one's young, for fear is identical with escape, whereas in the examples above the animal does not escape (as does the rabbit from the dog), but fights. And 'fighting', on the other hand, is identical with aggression (intraspecific fight). But perhaps the defence of one's young can be explained by 'love'? By no means, since love is identical with sexuality. Thus one of the greatest observers of nature in our time has elaborated a theory of instincts according to which the simplest, most commonly known or experienced facts become inexplicable.

The 'four basic instincts' defined in three ways in three different places lead to insoluble contradictions on other issues as well. Fear – to remain with drives and anthropomorphical thinking – is not always 'escape', not only because it can also find expression in combat, but also because, as we know, paralysing fear is not uncommon, a fear in which escape becomes impossible (it is by no means rarer than instraspecific fight.) If we identify 'love' with 'sexuality' then where do we place 'relations' between parent and offspring? (Of course, I am quite aware that these criticisms are also anthropomorphical, but I merely wish to show that Lorenz – even here – is incoherent.)

I do not mean to pretend that Lorenz considers the four basic instincts exclusive. For instance, he also speaks of a so-called 'ritualizational instinct', which may become powerful enough to repress the aforementioned basic instincts. In his theory the instinct of inhibition, primarily characteristic of the animals of prey, also plays a significant role: it is this instinct which prevents the instinct of aggression from leading to the extermination of the same species. But the basic instincts remain basic precisely

---

[35] Id., p. 84.
[36] Id., p. 100.

because they have an outstanding role in one respect: and these are common in man and animal, according to Lorenz. In the case of mankind the instinct of aggression leads to the physical extermination of specimens of his own species precisely because the instinct of inhibition is demolished as biological instinct along with the development of the use of tools, and is 'replaced' merely by social ritualization such as kneeling down, lifting the hand, crying, etc.[37] Thus the basic instincts, I repeat, are constructed on the basis of the ideological image of contemporary man and retrospectively built into animal behaviour as 'motives'.

Of course, Lorenz needs the homogenization of man's and animal's behaviour and system of motives from an opposite direction as well. For he wants to show that the 'aggressive instinct' is not something intrinsically 'evil', since it has a positive selective value in the world of animals (for instance, in the combat of the males the stronger triumphs, but the stronger is also better able to defend his offspring). Hence, according to Lorenz, there can be no doubt that the instinct of aggression also has a positive selective value with regard to man. (That in the case of animals he was dealing, according to his own admission, with one of the instincts of reproductive behaviour, whereas in the case of man he was dealing with combat between groups – is quite another matter.) In his analysis of the positive selective values Lorenz steps from the realm of the natural sciences into that of poetry of nature, for instance, when he writes: 'A personal bond, an individual friendship is found in animals with highly developed intra-specific aggression. . .'[38]

Furthermore, with regard to both animals and man: 'There is no love without aggression, but there is no hate without love.'[39] Furthermore, '. . . one can really hate only where one has loved and, even if one denies it, still does.'[40] I assume no one will doubt that the coral fish fighting for territory, or the bucks rivalizing for a female, 'love' each other as little as they 'hate' each other, not to mention the fact that the mixing together of aggression with hatred, as we shall see later on, is a mistake; it is a mistake with regard to man, since only mankind is capable of hatred. I do not question, furthermore, that man may hate the person he loved or he still loves (of course, the observation depends on our definition of 'love!'), but that we can only hate the person we love is a brash assertion that can be

---

[37] Several have rejected the theory of Lorenz according to which the instinct of inhibition has been demolished with the use of tools. Thus it is only carnivorous animals of prey that have an instinct of aggression, whereas the apes do not, and they do not even need it; in the case of man in formation (who, to judge by his dentition was omnivorous) it did not exist, and thus could not be demolished.

[38] Id., p. 209.

[39] *Id.,* p. 209.

[40] *Id.,*

formulated by 'ideologists of the instincts' only in the heat of passion of analysis. Thus, for instance, Lorenz proposed the construction of close rapports between humans as a means of avoiding the destructive consequences of aggression, forgetting that his theory does not allow for this: for the rapport breeds love, and love breeds hatred.

The 'genetical' grounding of the human 'instinct of aggression' in the world of animals leads to elementary contradictions and absurdities, which can be seen, I believe, through the foregoing examples. I will add only that on the last pages of Lorenz' work, naturally, we can already detect the contours of the symbolical catchphrase mentioned above. War, athletic activity, the struggle for scientific truth, enthusiasm in general – all appear as the derivatives of the 'instinct of aggression.'

Now let us take a brief look at the other typical tendency regarding the genesis of the instinct of aggression.

If I have spoken of 'poetry of nature' with reference to the late period of Lorenz, then I must use the term 'poetry' even more when describing what has been written about the formation of the instinct of aggression in the prehistory of man.[41] While the ethologists have the means to reduce poetry, the specialists in prehistory do not. The amount of data at their disposal is so meagre, the findings until the time of the appearance of the *Homo sapiens diluvialis* are so sparse, that historical reconstruction is impossible without a series of hypotheses and constructs.

What are the facts on which the reconstructions are based?

1. Some of the skulls of Australopithecus unconvered during diggings show indications of wounds caused by tools, among which a number were undoubtedly mortal. These wounds could only have been caused by hominides. In some places they have also uncovered the traces of cannibalistic meals. 2. Sinanthropic man (Pekin Man) has been found with similar skull wounds. 3. Finally, there is the so-called finding at Krapina: the remnants of a cannibalistic meal, where the ingredients of the feast were furnished by Neanderthal man.

These findings point to two unquestionable facts: 1. The human species we consider our ancestors did kill human beings, that is, they did not have intraspecific inhibitions, as predators do. 2. These same ancestors of ours consumed human flesh, that is 'intraspecific inhibition' was missing in this regard as well (on the other hand, think of the wolf, which is incapable of eating the meat of conspecifics and prefers to die of starvation). But these

---

[41] I evaluate as clearly negative the poetry of nature of the 20th century only if it pretends to appear as specialized knowledge. If it does not do this – or if I judge it from another point of view, – my estimate may be positive. Thus, for instance, I may consider Freud's description of the Ego struggling between the Superego and the Id as a moving phenomenological description in the manner of Flaubert, a description of the very typical status of modern man in the past century.

are the only facts, and every theory based upon these is mere hypothesis, reconstruction as, indeed, it can be nothing else.[42] The auxiliary interpretation, the sources of which are the most 'primitive' tribes of today – or rather of yesterday – can only be accepted critically and with qualifications, inasmuch as the most 'primitive', let us say Australian aborigines, present the man of *today* living at the cultural level of the late paleolithic. As we shall see, the anthropologists do not agree whether the 'instinct of aggression' exists everywhere; but beyond a doubt, homicide is not universal, and cannibalism is even rarer.

But let us take a brief look at the theory.

Eibl-Eibesfeld asserts the following: '. . .both aggressive and altruistic behaviour are pre-programmed by philogenetic adaptations.'[43] He believes it possible that these behaviours are of animal origin, but theoretically it is impossible to prove this:

> In animals all we can do is to note purely descriptively either the individualized striving for contact and a bond or alternatively aggression. Statements about the emotions that go with such behaviour are fundamentally impossible for epistemological reasons.[44]

According to him aggressivity evolved from rivalizing behaviour at the time of the formation of the human species, and became one of the dominating instincts. Proof of its instinctual nature: it is species-specific (there is no human being without aggression), and the human species is not 'malleable' in this regard.

Undoubtedly Eibl-Eibesfeld is the disciple of Lorenz from one aspect: he derives aggression from intra-specific fight. He rejects the overwhelming majority of pertinent theories which have pointed to hunting as the 'source' of this instinct. Thus, from a certain point of view, he leaves the facts even further behind than the other interpretations regarding the origins of the human 'instinct of aggression'. For we do know that prehistoric men hunted, but we do not know, and theoretically will never find out, whether he was prone to 'rivalizing behaviour' or not. The fact that the cannibalism of contemporary man-eating tribes has nothing to do with 'rivalizing behaviour' may still prove nothing to the contrary, it nevertheless places another question mark next to the conception of Eibl-Eibesfeld.

---

[42] That the findings provide but a very insecure foundation for reconstruction is shown by the following example from the area of tool usage, which is an area where 'more exact' measurements can be taken: it is well known that the axes from the period of the upper paleolithic are almost exactly identical wherever they have been found. According to the assumption of Movius, however, this is not sufficient proof that all tools used at the time were identical, for it is possible that modern-day researcher is simply unable to recognize tools that differ.

[43] Iräncus Eibl-Eibesfeld, *Love and Hate*, Methuen Co. Ltd., London, 1971, p. 4.

[44] Eibl-Eibesfeld, *op. cit.*, p. 6.

I have said that the majority of researchers consider hunting to be the original source of the human instinct of aggression.[45] Again I will select but one work for my analysis, the excellent book of Gottfried Kurth titled *Implications of Primate Paleontology for Behaviour*.

The hypotheses of Kurth are very important from my point of view. For whereas he does not distinguish clearly between the instinctive act, and the internal stimulus (drive) of the instinctive act, it is possible to interpret his arguments in this sense; and thus we are given a clue (if not the key!) for the true understanding of the phenomena of human aggressivity, to be sure, on the basis of my own theoretical preference.

First of all Kurth does not doubt that the repeated use of tools led to increasing malleability of behaviour, something that could only take place along with the instinct demolition. Plasticity '...became possible only because those portions of innate behaviour that were important for intra-specific behaviour had decreased. .'[46] He concludes from this that the first instincts to be demolished must have been the ones that insured the co-existence of the group and the positive selection of the species vis-a-vis nature; these were replaced, albeit very slowly, together, and simul-taneously by the social sphere and by work. (The duration of the process is a matter of some two million years.) At the same time the instinct demolition was not proportionate: '...the innate or instinctive modes of behaviour for propagation and the first stage after birth seem to have remained more or less unweakened ...'[47] Of course, one can speak of the appearance of man only once the instincts have also been demolished in the abovementioned areas, when these too become 'socialized', when here too the 'hiatus' comes about. For us it is important, in this demolition taking place in consecutive phases, that homicide interpreted as aggres-sivity (in early cannibalism) cannot result from 'rivalizing behaviour'. In the case of mammals, particularly of monkeys, rivalizing behaviour never leads to killing, whereas the first proof of early cannibalism is the Austra-lopithecus.[48]

But it is precisely from the sphere where, according to him, the instinct demolition or the process of self-domestication takes place the soonest that Kurth derives the extraordinary growth of the so-called 'instinct of aggression' as an internal stimulus. 'With such irregular amounts of food on the average, it must have been crucial for the hunter that his body could

[45] Among the authors I am familiar with, see the works of Dart and Arcley.
[46] Gottfried Kurth, *Implications of Primate Paleontology for Behaviour,* ed. J. N. Spuhler, in *Genetic Diversity and Human Behaviour,* Chicago: Aldine, 1967, p. 207.
[47] Kurth, *op. cit.,* p. 207.
[48] Kurth reached this conclusion on the basis of skull findings, with an assumed degree of cerebration.

release large, if short, bursts of energy, even though his state of nutrition was bad after a long period of hunger.'[49] Furthermore:

> In any case, we may expect that selection pressure acted through millions of years in the same direction, that is, to free by appropriate stimuli all available funds of energy in the human body. . . During the long life in small bands with very low population density, these outbursts of energy most likely had no dangerous consequences within the 'society'. This has probably changed ever since permanent settlement, intentional food production and increased population number have heightened the possibilities for tension.'[50]

The idea, I believe, is clear enough. Precisely because human beings are not specialized, because even with the help of primitive tools they had the capacity to fight against any animal species plasticity, and precisely because their instincts, as movement coordinations, have been demolished from the aspect of the way of food-procuring, furthermore, because this food, particularly in the ice-age, became sparse, for these reasons human beings needed an increase in the quantity of internal stimuli. This quantity of internal stimuli did not turn upon his own 'society', because he needed it in the 'struggle for existence' against other species. Hence man did not kill man because he had the instinct of aggression, but rather because he disposed of powerful, but not specific, internal stimuli, while he has no instincts.

But even this interpretation – the materials of which were taken from Kurth, but the conclusions being my own – warrants several question marks. On one hand I must question, whether we have the right to relate the powerful internal stimulus precisely with aggression, or to tie it up with aggression rather than anything else, whatever the prehistorical origins. Furthermore (and this is another aspect of the same question), whether I have the right to relate aggression to powerful internal stimuli. I just happen to raise the issue here, since I will have occasion to return to an analysis of rage and of functional independence.

Cannibalism must be discussed separately. There is only one connection between the general problem of homicide and the particular problem of cannibalism: man must be killed in order to be eaten.[51] The instinct demolition is also a prior condition of cannibalism, as it is a prior condition of homicide, but there is no necessary connection between the two. The essence of present-day (or yesterday's) cannibalism is not to consume human flesh, but rather a regulated magic rite tied to the most varied spiritual notions. It may vary according to whether or not it is related to

---

[49] Kurth, *Op. cit.,* 212.
[50] *Ibid.*
[51] Even here, not always. In some cases the object of ritualistic cannibalism is a deceased relative or member of the tribe.

individuals within the tribe or outside the tribe. Linton describes the cannibalism of the inhabitants of the Marquesas as affecting only those outside the tribe; within the tribe they reject not only the consumption of human flesh, but even killing with dread. The Tiv 'flesh-debt', however, according to the account given by Margaret Mead, is intra-tribal cannibalism. This latter is clearly of magical provenance in all respects. About the former Linton says that the consumption of male prisoners is regulated by magic rites, whereas that of women and children is free of all rites: these are consumed merely because the taste is appreciated. I must draw attention to yet another, in my opinion important, difference between homicide and cannibalism: the so-called powerful internal stimulus which Kurth mentions and which played such an important role in hunting, hence probably in the hunting of man where such a thing existed, has no role whatever in cannibalism, and indeed it has presumably no role in a number of magic rites the essence of which is homicide (human sacrifice). The gods usually required the sacrifice not of the hated but of the most beloved beings.

It would be very difficult to derive conclusions from the types of cannibalism I am familiar with, regarding the prehistory of man. As Kurth writes:

> We must again refer to the outstanding 'human' characteristic, cannibalism. Its appearance underlines clearly enough the loss of innate standards maintained by instinctive, schematized behaviour. Indeed, it is unnecessary to emphasize that ethnologically known cannibalism with ritual or magic cannot be a model for the kind of cannibalism verified archaeologically for the early stages of human hominids by undoubted traces of the fossil remains. On the other hand, we may presuppose that a mutual social behaviour of group members must have been provided among the australopithecines through some – *cum grano salis* – social tradition.[52]

I must add that the idea expounded in the last sentence, which is undoubtedly a true statement, is no proof of the magic nature of ancient cannibalism.

## 2. THE BIO-PSYCHOLOGICAL EVIDENCE

Now let us turn to the examination of that 'inner stimulus', which Kurth regards as of positive selective value in the evolution of the human species.

This is all the more important since the theories of the 'instinct of

[52] Kurth, *Op. cot.*, p. 208.

aggression' make appeal as proof to a single clearly existing *biological* fact[53] that is not a working hypothesis: anger. All their other references are definitely of a social nature.

It is Bain who presents the most fruitful summary of the notions of anger contained in the theories of the instinct of aggression. According to this: 'Like a steam boiler, man has a certain load of pressure, and where this energy goes, depends on what valves are habitually open.'[54] According to this theory, such an increase in the inner pressure of impulses that has to be acted out compulsively, is specifically characteristic of the human species, what more, in some type of act of destruction. What specific channels this destructive energy will take depends on the social sphere: it may be war, duel, witchhunt, the burning of heretics, and even self-torture or the smashing of vases. Following Freud the 'release' of this destructive energy is also called catharsis. The catharsis liberates the individual from the pressure of the inner 'steam', until steam-pressure accumulates anew and the person must once again release it through the available channels. Several advocates of this theory have ascribed the effect of fascism on the masses to the fact that modern existence provides few such channels, and the 'steam' can never be completely released, thus considerable tension is created, and people await with anxiety situations in which this steam can be released through any channel, but preferably through the most extreme channel of destruction, homicide.[55]

Since the production of internal stimuli – the biological source of anger – is an undeniable fact; furthermore, it is also undeniable that these stimuli must find release, I cannot deny the relative validity of Bain's hypothesis. Everybody knows, from empirical experience, that if certain stimuli accumulate, i.e. cannot find release for a prolonged period, the eventual release will assume more violent, more intense forms. Yet the formulation of this fact as a general law, its specific application to aggression, furthermore the derivation of aggression and its intensity solely from the quantity of pressure accumulated, has been greeted with scepticism by many. I will repeat a few of the objections here (Kuo, Allport, Newcomb) briefly. While undoubtedly there are internal stimuli which may lead to fits of rage, on one hand the quantity of stimulus varies from individual to individual, on the other this same quantity is not unrelated to outside factors, it cannot simply be ascribed to the con-

[53] I will attempt to prove later on that even human anger is not merely a biological fact. I will use the terms 'anger' and 'rage' alternately and consider them to be expressions of the same bio-psychological process. Differentiation will only be made between them in a social context of rationality or irrationalitly ascribed to them.
[54] M. G. Allport, *Pattern and Growth in Personality*, New York: Holt, Rinehart, and Winston, 1961, p. 52.
[55] The description is valid for certain, or even numerous individuals.

sequences of some internal secretion. Even animals can be trained to become aggressive by insuring victory to them. The successful release not only prompts the repeated use of the same channel of release, but also increases the production of internal stimulus. Thus rats may be trained to become enraged by insuring them successful release. This is even more applicable to the case of man. The living out of anger not only releases the accumulated pressure (although it certainly does), but also plays a part in what sort of stimulus pressures will be produced in the future. The decrease in the number of channels of release, or their total lack, may lead not only to the production of stimulus pressure 'ready to' explode, but also to a decrease in the pressure of the stimulus. Human beings are capable – at least many of them – of keeping their stimuli 'to themselves' (Gehlen), and this is precisely the source of human inwardness. Keeping the stimulus to oneself may not only lead to the greater intensity of the eventual explosion of tension, but may also lead to the omission of the explosion. At the same time the channels of the stimuli are not necessarily acts of aggression. When an angry person releases or sublimates his anger by counting to thirty, or by going for a walk, then the release does not pertain to anger, not even if there had been a sufficient amount of 'stimulus pressure'.

I quote the definition of anger from Henry Murray (*Studies of Stressful Interpersonal Disputations*), since he lists every one of its aspects that are important for my analysis. According to this definition, anger is nothing but an

hypothetical state of excitation in certain not-yet-definitely-localized, sub-cortical regions of the brain (say, in the hypothalamus and limbic systems) which, if sufficiently intense, produces various manifestations of which the following will be discriminated in our data.
1) Covert manifestations: experienced or felt anger, aggressive words or images, etc.
2) Physiological manifestations: autonomic excitation, including changes of the heart rate and respiration.
3) Overt manifestations: physiognomic and motoric phenomena – verbal productions. . . vocal qualities.

And he adds:

. . . everything modulated to some degree by the subject's efforts to control and to conceal them.[56]

We can only speak of anger if all the factors listed by Murray are present jointly.

Before turning to the analysis and elaboration of the symptoms given in

[56] Henry Murray, *Studies of Stressful Interpersonal Disputations* in *Theories of Personality*, eds. Lindsay and Hall, New York-London-Sydney: J. Wiley and Sons, 1965, p. 180.

the definition, I would like to draw a conclusion very decisive for us from the statement above: if the presence of all the factors listed is necessary in order to be able to speak of anger, then the acts of aggression of destruction cannot be derived from anger since they are in no way related. Hence the sole biological factor as demonstration of aggression, from the point of view of an important group of aggressions, proves to be irrelevant.

For the sake of simplicity let us take a literary example. Richard the Third hires two murderers to kill his younger brother Prince Clarence. When Richard assigns the commission, at least two of the three symptoms of anger are definitely missing. He acts in cold blood, and nothing indicates a 'state of excitation' in him. Undoubtedly, neither does his breathing become more rapid, nor does the production of his hormones change. If we examined his physiognomy – and, indeed, this is how every actor acts out the scene – we would only note expressions of pleasure, glee, success, plotting, victory, determination. Without a doubt, he does not blush, does not pale, and does not tremble. (Incidentally, this same Richard is particularly proud of the fact that in order to attain a certain goal he can manipulate a fit of rage without actually feeling anger.) Now let us recall what the two murderers feel before and during the execution of their assignment. The first is psychologically indifferent, he is an 'artisan' of murder, for him it is a matter of routine. In Shakespeare's description the other murderer's state of mind is characterized by the feeling of pity. He is only inclined to execute the act when his accomplice reminds him of the expected high reward. Thus, in this case, aggression was clearly motivated by interest. One might say that among Shakespeare's heroes it is rather the ones with a noble soul who kill out of raging passion (Mercutio, Romeo or Othello). Quite often, however, those with an obviously angry and passionate disposition do not kill (Lear). The ones who kill do it out of the most varied motivations which may be, in some cases, free of passion, and in others communicated by passions other than anger. For instance, Brutus kills out of virtue, Macbeth out of desire for power, and out of fear, Hamlet as a matter of chastisement, and Richard III, Edmund, or Iago, out of frustration – although these latter have rather people killed than kill themselves.

I believe this should be already sufficient to prove the thesis that the most extremely aggressive act, the annihilation of another human being, is not at all in necessary connection with the sole biological fact the believers in the theory of the instinct of aggression have used to justify the existence of that instinct. But all this does not pertain simply to the extreme manifestation of aggression. The parent who considers corporal punishment an excellent means of education, hits most of the time in cold blood, without any anger. One person may shout at another not only because of anger, but may do so intentionally: in order to intimidate, in order to make him to shut up, or even to keep the other person from some fateful act. The cousin may have fantasies about the death of his uncle without any anger involved; they may not even be acquainted, the cousin may simply want to inherit the wealth. The businessman may ruin his competitor without any feeling of anger either because he does not want to get ruined himself or because he wants to obtain greater profits (again, possibly, without being acquainted with his competitor). And the examples can be multiplied. Of course, all this does not mean that I want to deny the significance of anger in eliciting certain types of behaviour that may be qualified as aggressive, it only means that in my opinion there is no necessary and generalizable connection between anger and the act of aggression, the former does not necessarily motivate the latter, whereas the latter is not necessarily motivated by the former.

Let me raise, however, another question: is it always anger that motivates the action in case the anger stimulus is obviously present and indeed finds an outlet in the given act? To answer this question we may find guidance in everyday word usage... When do we say 'I did this or that out of rage' or 'he did what he did out of rage'? Exclusively if the action contradicts or bothers our preference of values. If someone should step on our toes and we respond with a slap in the face, and we should explain that we did it out of rage, then what we mean is this: if I had the chance for a well considered act, if I I had not been overcome by passion, then I would have acted differently, and I regret having slapped him. If a parent who considers corporal punishment acceptable or valuable and who slaps his son, because his son told a lie, will not say, 'I did out of rage.', but rather that 'I was angry.'. Anger as opposed to rage means, to use a behaviourist expression, that this was the adequate response to the stimulus (the lie). If a parent who despises corporal punishment resorts to this means, then he will say 'I did it out of rage', not because he does not condemn lying but because it is not corporal punishment he regards as an adequate response to that particular stimulus. If someone should see a man strangling a child and strikes the man to save the child, he will by no means say 'I did it out of rage.' but rather 'I did out of indignation.'. If my superior should act unjustly towards someone and I should give him a piece of my mind and resign, later 1) if I should feel I had acted rightly I will have to say I acted out of anger and indignation, but 2) if I should regret it later, I will have to say that I acted out of rage.

I do not have the space to analyse the differences in the meaning of rage, anger, indignation, vengeance, etc. – (among other things, this is the reason why I mostly use the last two terms indiscriminately). Yet I think this is sufficient to make clear that 'rage' has social implications even in everyday word usage: even here we do not consider it spontaneously as a mere biological phenomenon.

Now let us return to a more detailed analysis of certain aspects of Murray's definition.

Let us examine, first of all, the biological and physiological factors jointly, – that is the state of excitation that comes about in the subcortical regions – furthermore the physiological symptoms summarized in Murray's second point. I must add that, in the unanimous opinion of biologists this so-called state of excitation corresponds to an increase in hormone production or, in another formulation, increase in hormone production is the state of excitation (secretion of ACTH or of TSH – whereas Funkenstein observed a strong secretion of norepinefrine) and, many have noted among the physiological symptoms an increase in blood pressure, a rise in the level of blood sugar.

No doubt such a state of excitation exists and can be experimentally verified. Yet I must ask two questions. The first is, can that state of excitation be specific for anger, in other words, is there a kind of excitation which only appears along with the other symptoms ascribed to anger? The other questions goes as follows: is it purely a matter of internal stimulus produced in greater degree by the hypothalamus, and which merely awaits an opportunity for release through some 'vent' under the impact of some external stimulus, when the 'vent' plays a secondary function with regard to the stimulus, or the appearance of the stimulus (and its content) is itself socially codetermined? To express the question biologically: does the cortex affect the appearance of such a stimulus in the hypothalamus, and does it affect the degree of its appearance?

Let us examine the first question.

Stanley Schachter, an outstanding experimental researcher of these processes, clearly denies the affect specific character of stimuli. Nor is he the first to do so; he follows in the footsteps of Cannon, Maranon, Cantril, Hunt, Landis, Lindsley and others. Cannon had already determined that 'the same visceral changes occur in very different emotional states and in nonemotional states. . .[57] I should add that Murray, who provided the initial definition, also agrees: and this is the reason why the considers the symptoms he listed as the specific manifestation of anger only if they all appear together.

Mandis and Hunt had injected adrenalin into 210 patients, and then requested them to give an account of their sensations. 71% of the patients reported only physiological symptoms, whereas the other 29% as follows: 'I feel as if I were afraid.', 'I feel as if I were enraged.', 'I feel as if I were happy.', etc. The physiological symptoms corresponded to those described by Murray and others. But the majority perceived them merely as physio-

[57] Quoted in Stanley Shachter, 'A Cognitive-Psychological View of Emotion' in *Perspectives in Social Psychology*, New York: Holt, Rinehart, and Winston, 1965, 75.

logical symptoms, and even the minority described them as analogical to feelings only because they lacked the social-cognitive mediating cause which would elicit an affect from the given stimulus. The description by means of analogies to feelings is significant because the patients referred to a diversity of passions or feelings, which is proof enough that the biological stimulus itself is not specific.

Schachter has also carried out other experiments, more complex, and even more interesting for our point of view. The subjects were not told what kind of hormone injections they were administered. Then they lived through various situations. They were shown erotic movies, movies replete with episodes of aggression, or took part in aesthetic experiences. Those who watched erotic films felt a strong sexual urge, those who watched aggressive films or those who felt frustrated in their efforts at competition felt rage, whereas those who were exposed to aesthetic experiences showed pleasure, along with their mimic symptoms: these were the feelings they reported later, and these were the feelings they expressed in their 'overt behaviour' (from fighting to erotic propositions). All this demonstrated clearly that even the artificial reinforcement of the stimulus formed in the hypothalamus creates but an 'opportunity' for the actual provocation of a number of rather distinct affects. What affect comes about is not determined in the biological 'stimulus'.

Schachter arrives at far-reaching and rather significant conclusions from all this, and I accept these conclusions. He summarizes them as follows: 'cognitive factors may be the major determinants of emotional states.'[58]

It follows from all this that there is no biological stimulation that stimulates rage specifically. Let us recall now the conception elaborated by Kurth regarding the formation of the so-called 'instinct of aggression' in the prehistory of mankind. Prehistorical man, in order to maintain himself successfully as a hunter, needed a strong dose of impulse. But if we accept Schachter's assertion, as I have done, then it does not follow that this strong dose of impulse can only find an outlet in acts of an aggressive character. I do not want to repeat what I have already stated, that there is aggression without rage, but simply that the strong impulse itself does not necessarily 'appear' in the form of the affect of 'rage', but may appear under other forms (along with their symptoms). In this case the interpretation of Kurth does not answer the question why human beings have strong 'instincts of aggression', but rather why do they have strong basic affects in general.

I believe that on the basis of all this it is already possible to answer the second question I have raised. The specific nature of the stimulus is a function of the social-cognitive situation. If we have accepted this much,

---

[58] Schachter, in *op. cit.*, p. 76.

then the problem whether the quantity of stimulus is also a function of the cognitive-social sphere or not becomes essentially irrelevant from the point of view of our question (the plasticity of man, the potential of his nature for building in various factors.) For the type of human being who is 'free of strong affects' is very far from being my ideal. I must add, however, that there are theories which claim that this quantity is also determined. For instance, Homburg and Lunde, in their *Relation of Behavioural, Genetic and Neuroendocrine Factors to Thyroid Function* analyse how stress, elicited by social factors, brings about excessive activity of the thyroid gland, hence a higher degree of irritability on the part of the entire organism; in other words, stress derived from social conflicts increases the quantity of stimuli. The production of stimuli of not cerebral origin is communicated or at least influenced by processes that take place in the brain, primarily in the cortex. The aggressivity stemming from frustration, to be analysed later in this treatise, cannot be explained any other way. For frustration is the blocking of our end-oriented activities, and this process, as all teleological and related events, can be located in the cortex.

With a witty and seemingly convincing example Lorenz attempts to demonstrate the instinctive nature of the quantity of internal aggressive stimulus. The larger the quantity of internal stimulus, the smaller the external stimulus needed for eliciting the instinctive act. An example of this is the so-called polar disease. Polar explorers who during a protracted period live away from the 'normal' stimuli of society in isolation, break out, as is well known, in fits of rage at the slightest stimulus. They practically seek those stimuli to which they may react with rage, for instance those habits of their companions which, under normal circumstances, would not elicit any kind of violent reaction. The description of the phenomenon seems apt enough, and perhaps we need not go as far as the explorer to be convinced. But the phenomenon is no evidence at all as to the existence of the quantity of internal stimuli constantly in production. Let us recall the facts mentioned above, according to which a stress situation increases internal irritability. I believe no one would question that isolation from society constitutes a stress situation, not to mention the tasks requiring considerable efforts on the part of the polar explorer, the constant presence of mortal danger, etc.

But let us continue our analysis of the definition by Murray. I am going to discuss the so-called 'covert' manifestations referred to under number one together, and the so-called 'overt' manifestations mentioned under number three – the organic constituents of rage.

I will discuss these two points together because it is only in the presence of both that we may speak of anger. The anger that exists only as inner 'feeling' is not anger from the point of view of its social import; we can only call anger the situation to which the environment may react as such.

In fact, apart from introspection, there is no way of making assertions regarding the presence or absence of such anger. As a minimum, anger must be present in the mimicry which expresses its repression in order to be understood as anger.

Nor can we consider as rage that which appears merely in external manifestations. It is well known that there are 'daytime actors' who are capable of manipulated fits of rage, that is, who are capable of playing the symptoms of rage without actually feeling rage. (Let us recall once again the example of Richard the Third.) Of course, socially we must consider this type of feeling as anger, particularly if it is expressed in types of action that are characteristic of anger, since the other person reacts to manipulated fits of rage, in general, as he would to genuine rage. As Bedford writes:

> If a man who is behaving as if he were angry goes so far as to smash the furniture or commit an assault, he has passed the limits; he is not pretending and it is useless for him to protest afterwards that he did not feel angry.[59]

An exception might be someone we know quite well and if we know that his fits of rage are manipulated. I should add, however, that a consistently performed 'daytime acting', at least in this regard, is very rare. Innumerable social psychologists have analysed the fact that mimicry of anger and gestures of anger may also become stimuli to anger. 'Its practice' is capable of arousing the feeling of anger. It is not only the blow that elicits anger, but also the act of hitting may itself elicit its 'inner awareness' of anger. 'Even the simulation of an emotion tends to arouse it in our minds.' wrote Darwin.[60]

Regarding the 'external manifestations' of rage we must differentiate between two 'groups', and rather sharply at that. The one contains the expressions of rage in gesture and mimicry, and the other the types of behaviour and coordinations of movement expressed in the actions provoked by rage. The differentiation is important to us, because the expressions of rage, as we shall see later, are provided in the genetic code and are species-specific, whereas the types of behaviour and coordinations of movement differ according to culture and to individual; they have no biological determination.

Even Darwin described the expressions of rage in his brilliant book titled *The Expression of the Emotions in Man and Animals*. These include the following: 'retraction of the lips and uncovering the teeth', 'the reddening

---

[59] E. Bedford, 'Emotions', in *Essays in Philosophical Psychology*, ed. Donald Gustafson, New York: Doubleday, 1964, p. 82.
[60] Charles Darwin, *The Expression of the Emotions in Man and Animals*, London: John Murray, 1872, p. 366.

of the face', but 'the heart is sometimes so much impeded by great rage, that the countenance becomes pallid or livid', 'such gestures as the raising of the arms, with the fists clenched .. are common', 'trembling is a frequent consequence of rage'.[61] Some among these are in common between man and his ape ancestors – the uncovering of the canine teeth, stamping, or shaking – in fact, they may be encountered, one by one, among other higher species of mammals. Darwin analysed the genesis of the uncovering of canine teeth which, as indeed it seems likely, is the remnant of movement coordination of 'being ready to bite', that is an instinct remnant. Paling, reddening, and trembling are of compulsive force, that is they cannot be regulated by self-control, by an effort of the will. Yet reddening and paling are peculiarly human expressions, since these require a face, and only human beings have a face. The other 'expressions' of rage, to which we may add a few, may be regulated by the will, but this regulation is itself compulsorily expressed in mimicry: for instance if, instead of shaking the fist threateningly, we should keep our clenched fist close to our body, or if instead of shouting we keep a stiff upper lip, etc.

The innate aspect of expression of rage does not reside in the fact that all its symptoms can be observed among all persons in a state of rage. Different expressions characterize different persons, and the expressions may even vary within the same individual according to the nature of the stimulus provoking rage. But some symptom, or some symptom of the 'repression' of symptoms, must be present. Furthermore, these symptoms are not characteristic of a specific culture, but may be observed at whole mankind regardless of the content or stage of development, etc., of the culture. Thus, if a person is enraged, then this necessarily 'appears' in some expression characteristic of rage.

Let us now turn to a different theme, to the acts of anger. Since human beings, to use Gehlen's expression, are 'open beings', there is not a single movement coordination that would be species-specific with regard to action. Anger itself does not in the least determine the nature of the acts, of the coordination of movements, or of a sequence of these in which it will find release. Consider killing. This has only one 'natural' manner given by the human organism, that is to beat somebody to death. Hence Schopenhauer defined man as the 'beating animal'. (Because of the lack of differentiation of the paw the animal cannot beat to death.) But if man kills by means of poison, arrows, the sword, revolver, gun-barrel, stone, or atomic bomb, rather than mere hands and physical force, then his coordination of movement (and indeed the series of actions in general) must be adapted to the tool with which he kills. A tool comes between

---

[61] Darwin, op. cit., pp. 239, 40-41.

him and the object of his rage, the existence, hence use of which is socially determined. In order for someone to pull out his sword, to reach to his holster, or point his bayonet, it is not enough to be 'enraged', he must first acquire the 'aptitude' to use the sword, the revolver, or the bayonet. (And, as we have seen, it is possible to use all these instruments without being enraged.) Even the recourse to the kind of tools or weapons is socially determined, often according to social class or strata. (Even today it is 'proper' to shoot the soldier to death rather than to hang him.)

Cursing or invectives are typical acts of speech resulting from anger. (Yet again one may curse coolly, without rage.) The formula for cursing are socially regulated and differ depending on who it is used against. Thus one may not shout at a man that he is a whore or a bitch. It is once again in Shakespeare that we may find the most striking examples of the general formula of cursing and invective, and the 'combination' of its individually characterized forms: witness the scene in which Queen Margaret damns Richard and his kin.

I have stated, regarding the act of instinct, that the same stimulus elicits the same coordination of movement. Of course, if the stimulus is identical that does not yet imply that the object is the same. For instance, Tinbergen has described the behaviour of species of fish who react aggressively against members of their own species. As it turned out from his experiments, these fish reacted to the perception of the red colour of their stomach. Artificial fish of the same shape did not elicit the appropriate reaction, whereas other 'imitations of fish', the forms of which differed considerably from the form of the species, yet had their nether side painted in red, did elicit the same aggressive coordination of movements. The bull reacts with a fit of rage to blood or to red felt alike. All this does not refute but confirms the identity of stimuli.

In the case of man, therefore, we must ask: do identical (or similar) 'stimuli'[62] bring about identical (or similar) types of reaction?

Let us take the case of someone hurt in his dignity. (Placing into parentheses what is considered an attack against one's dignity, since this varies greatly.) In such cases the aboriginal inhabitants of the Trobriand Islands, as we learn from Malinowski, climb up a tree and commit suicide. The medieval noblemen challenges his offender to a duel. Certain British citizens write indignant letters to the editor of the *Times*. Thus it is not merely the coordination of movements that differs, but even the social content of the action differs qualitatively. It is clear that in the reactions to similar feelings (or to occasions eliciting those feeling) cultural expectations and individual dispositions play equally important roles, what

---

[62] I place the term 'stimulus' between commas, for here it is mainly a matter of affects, or of moods and emotions reintegrating cognition.

more: the individual disposition and morality assume increasing importance in our time.

Since we unavoidably evaluate in our judgments, we could never place and never do place an equality sign between differing responses to identical stimuli, affects, or feelings. Since our value judgments vary according to culture and individual moral choice, we will differ in which reactions to deem correct, praiseworthy, and which to be condemned. There were times when to react to the faithlesness of a wife in the lofty manner of Anatole France's M. Bergeret would have been the 'sign' of cowardice rather than that of spiritual nobility. Nowadays it is this type of 'response' we consider noble and adequate, and there is nothing we condemn more strongly than killing for the sake of jealousy (of course, as we know even today this is not the case in certain civilized countries such as Southern Italy). If somebody should react to a personal offence by reporting the incident to the police, we would consider and judge this to be more despicable than if he were to respond with a slap in the face, whereas we would not condemn him morally if the offended party should bang the table in his rage. And, what is decisive for our purpose, the manner of response changes culturally typically in proportion to the widespread extension of the evaluation of one 'manner of response' or another.

What does all this mean in terms of the malleability (plasticity) of man? Even if we should assume (what I have not assumed), that there is a specific stimulus of anger, even if we should assume (what, as we have seen, I have not assumed) that man is a 'boiler' from which the constantly produced steam must be released again and again through one vent or another, even in such cases we cannot conclude to the existence of an 'instinct of aggression' which necessarily plays a role in social relations, and which is directed at the destruction or harming of another human being. Because if this pressure of anger can be released by smashing an object to pieces, by banging on the table, by raising the voice, as well as by killing a person, by humiliating him, by scourging him, or by trampling him, then this stimulus may become socially indifferent provided that the other kinds of 'release' are condemned to such an extent that the overwhelming majority is not inclined to resort to it.

Thus far I have examined the relationship 'similar stimuli – different response'. Now let me take a look at the relationship 'different stimuli – similar response'. Thus I may react similarly to an offense against my particular being, against a principle, against a value, against the weaker, etc.

The adherents of the instinct-drive theory would, of course, reply that in these cases it is merely the occasion or situation eliciting the external stimulus that varies, but that the internal stimulus remains the same. This is undoubtedly a justified objection, at least as far as anger is concerned.

What I mean to say is simply that the external 'stimulus' may fill not only the function of 'vent' for the channel of release, but also participates in the determination of the degree of intensity, or the 'formation' of the internal stimulus according to the values and norms of the individual.

But I must call attention to another important aspect of the matter, 'differing stimuli'. And this is that often human rage is not at all directed against the stimulus that has elicited it. It is often not even a human being that has elicited rage. Thus we may discuss to what extent rage may be a typical response in case of inability to solve a problem. (Köhler has already noted this phenomenon among apes.) The common characteristic of this event and of similar ones is that the stimulus responds to something to which we cannot respond with an action, with a rational act. This kind of rage is the expression of impotence. Yet, even in these situations rage is not the only possible specific stimulus. In the same situation we may find release in crying or laughter. The child unable to solve a mathematical problem may 'respond' to his or her inability by a fit of rage or by crying. If we are harmed by powers whose force surpasses ours manifold, against which we are unable to fight or to act, then we may respond with rage, with plaintive crying, or with a laugh; what more, one 'type of reaction' may well spill into another, our rage may turn into laughter or crying, or vice-versa, demonstrating the undetermined nature of the internal stimulus and the 'response'.

Remember our premise: the theories of the instinct of aggression are all drive theories. According to these theories the instinct of aggression is the motive, incentive, or energy source of our actions. Let us recall, furthermore, that the sole biological fact (or at least the only factor that has a biological aspect) pertinent to the instinct of aggression is anger. The arguments expounded above were meant to introduce scepticism in this regard. For I have shown regarding a significant type of rage that it is not a drive, not a motive, not a source of energy leading to action, but precisely a block to action, the expression of the incapacity to react, of impotence. Let us now take another step along this road.

Every advocate of the theory of drives considers each drive as a need as well. If we refine this conception and assert that hunger is a drive, whereas feeding is a need, then I will accept this argument. In both cases we have asserted that the preservation of mankind unquestionably demands that the various cultures should insure the continuity, the security of feeding and reproduction, albeit in various ways. But what sense does it make to pretend that anger (since it is the only biologically relevant factor of aggression), or fear are needs? That without their satisfaction, modified according to the culture, humanity would not be able to preserve itself? Once again we may discern here that already mentioned unconscious 'reversal' according to which everything that plays a part in human civilization today is undoubtedly a need of mankind, hence it is drive, motive, or energy. So, it turns out that the basis of the 'drives' of fear and of anger, as biological needs, does not reside in biological facts, but on arbitrarily interpreted social observations. What are the social facts which have provided a basis for this theory of needs?

# II THE NATURALIST THEORY OF THE INSTINCT OF AGGRESSION

## 3) THE SOCIAL EVIDENCES

Now let us return to the already mentioned all-inclusive bag into which the advocates of the theory of the instinct of aggression have stuffed those social actions, relations, institutions, character traits, types of reaction, forms of objectivation which they have deemed of the same gender as attributes of 'aggression'. My book would remain forever incomplete if I only analysed the majority of them. Let me lift out of the bag, therefore, those facts which I feel to be the most solid, which seem best to support the theories regarding the existence of the instinct of aggression, the theories it is my intention to refute.

The first fact I picked out is war as 'institution', usually considered the most natural vent or outlet channel of the instinct of aggression.[63]

The claim sounds as follows: the main proof of the existence of the instinct of aggression is that there has always been war, that war is species-specific, that it is an institution that exists among all groups of humans.

This claim cannot be demonstrated regarding prehistorical times, and even in our modern world there are 'primitive' tribes that do not know of war.

But let us suppose, however, that we are dealing with a species-specific institution, and let us examine briefly whether the fact of war proves the existence of the instinct of aggression.

Of course, I do not mean to deny that war indeed provides the occasion for the manifestation and release of aggression; I cannot deny that some of those who participate in war release their accumulated 'store of aggression' in killing and torture. I only mean to deny that we are dealing with some kind of 'instinct', that war in general is the 'vent' for the release of accumulated stores of aggression, furthermore, that the motive of war, and of the 'drive' that gives it birth and perpetuates it is aggressivity.

At the very starting point of my analysis we should take into consideration a well-known fact: in the overwhelming majority of cultures women do not participate in war. If war is the necessary 'vent' for the release of the

---

[63] For instance in the work of Kluckholn, *Mirror for Man.*

aggressive drive, then why does half of mankind not require such a vent? Must we assume that the drive of aggression is not species-specific, but only specific of the human male? Yet there have been cultures, however few, where women fought as well! Are we to assume that these women had the instinct of aggression, whereas the 'females' in other cultures did not? Of course, there are herds of monkeys where only the stronger males take part in combat; but among these the females never play a role in the fight – since we are talking of instinctive acts, albeit in the process of being demolished. In the case of humanity, however, participation in war is completely culturally determined. It is always the culture that determines who may participate in the fight, or who must participate therein, according to their physical strength, their skill, their sex or, quite often, according to their membership in a caste or an order. Or should we assume that, in bourgeois society, it is only since the introduction of universal military service that everyone has an instinct of aggression!

The drive-instinct theory could reply to all this that the 'vent' of war has been closed to women, hence they are forced to release their aggressivity through other 'vents'. This, however, already makes doubtful that war is a necessary vent in the release of the drive of aggression, not to mention that no one may claim that, since the vent of war is not open to women, they are more aggressive than men in other regards.

But to go a little further: if everyone – let it be only every human male – should have the instinct of aggression, which is of compulsive force as instinct, and which strives for release, then those who did not want to participate in wars could not have existed. Yet such people existed even among 'primitive' tribes where the norms prescribe activities uniformly, and where the opportunities for the development of the abilities of man are but very limited, and the social conditions for the acquisition of a 'personal' morality that would differ from the 'official' morality do not exist. Thus, even among a warlike tribe such as the Comanche there have always been men who did not want to participate in war, who do not feel competent to wage war. These are the so-called 'bedroche', who wear womanly attire, thus 'signaling' that they stay outside of military customs. Incidentally, in all other respect they were 'normal' (not homosexuals). In every civilized society there are masses of people who would do anything rather than make war. Newcomb has stated, with justified irony, that if the aggressive instinct really existed there would be no need to resort to capital punishment against deserters.

It may be objected, however, that in these cases it is not a matter of lack of instinct, but rather the repression of the instinct by morality. 'Do not kill,' the human child is taught, and this is what impedes him in 'living out' his instinct. I would reply that there are a number of moral and religious laws that sanction war, that encourage a fighting attitude, that even support ruthlessness in war. To participate in war is a merit, a duty, a virtue; it is praiseworthy to kill the enemy. It is hardly necessary to point to the scalps of the Indians, these decorations for 'nobility' and 'excellence' in war, it will suffice to quote from the same Bible whence the Western civilizations have taken the *mot d'ordre* 'do not kill'. Moses, who engraved the tablet on which the words 'do not kill' appear, gave the following instructions after defeating the Medes: 'Now therefore kill every male among the little ones, and kill every woman who has known man by lying with him.' (Moses IV, XXXI, 17) Or in the book of Samuel: 'Thus says the Lord of hosts. . . Now go and smite Amalek, and utterly destroy all that they have; do not spare them but kill both man and woman, infant and suckling, ox and sheep, camel and ass.' (Book of Samuel, I, XV, 3) And since Saul did not carry out the orders of the Lord a hundred percent, he had to be punished (and not because of the sins he committed against David). As the witch of Endor says: 'Because you did not obey the voice of the Lord and did not carry out his fierce wrath against Amalek, therefore the Lord has done this to you this day.' (Book of Samuel, I, XXVIII, 18) Why would it be necessary to repeat the command for the extermination of the progeny of the enemy, why would punishment have to be meted out in case of omission, if man were always willing and inclined to kill as a consequence of his 'instinct of aggression'?

I think I have proven with sufficient 'hard' facts that war is not an 'act of instinct', that killing in war is not the manifestation of a 'drive' having the force of compulsion. Let us then return to the other problem: whether war in general is indeed the vent of release for previously accumulated instincts of aggression?

I will not deny that this may apply to particular cases and that, indeed, these cases may be quite numerous. Probably the majority of those who enlisted voluntarily with the SS were prepared to kill. (But even here we must not forget about those who, when they later witnessed what was going on at the concentration camps, volunteered to go to the front.) But even if we admit the opportunity for 'releasing' accumulated aggressions in war, we must emphasize the opposite process as well: it is war itself, it is the 'freedom' to kill that continually gives birth to and produces aggression. In this 'inebriation with blood' aggressive impulses accumulate even among those who showed no traces of it earlier. Drives are not released through the permissible channels: drives are actually formed, or aroused in action. Even though it may sound frightening: it is objectivation that creates the need even in this case. When I have said that human nature, with respect to behaviour, is identical with what can be 'built in' man, then I have also said, by the same token, that aggression in its most extreme form may also become part of the nature of man, since it can be built into it. At the same time it cannot be built in if the structure of society does not provide the opportunity for 'objectivation'.

We must approach the theory regarding the release of 'accumulated aggression' with considerable caution since one of its main proofs, held to be of decisive importance, is the assertion that in times of war conflicts within the society weaken. We must be cautious if only because one of the presuppositions of this notion is that conflicts within society are manifestations of the aggressive instinct. I think it is superfluous to insist that these social conflicts are caused by the most varied social problems and disagreements rather than by the 'aggressive instincts'.

According to the theory of the instinct of aggression, war is brought about and maintained by the aggressive 'drive'.

The advocates of the theory of drives have often been accused of 'modernization'. I will repeat this suspicion and underline it. At the focus of the theory of the instinct of aggression we find, in usually explicit terms, the problem of the avoidability or inevatibility of war; the work of Mischerlich, for instance, bears the following revealing title: *Die Idee des Friedens und die menschliche Agressivität.*[64] Some vote for its avoidability, while others, referring to human nature, vote for the inevitability of war. But the issue itself, based as it is on the present condemns all wars with a clearly negative value accent – condemns war in general. More or less as follows: 'Whence does this calamity come?' I clearly expect the elimination of war right now and vote for a future that does not know war. But the negative assessment of war in general only makes sense (and I am not thinking of the negative assessment of certain specific wars) since unified humanity emerged – in concept if not in fact. This point of view, however, cannot be projected back into the past; it is not possible to describe war as some kind of an 'irrational' fact or institution originating in the dark world of human instincts and disturbing or hampering rational development.

I have no space to discuss war in general, I just want to assert clearly that the innumerable wars fought in the course of history have an inexhaustible and very heterogeneous number of specific causes. Even if I accepted the theory of drives (as I do not), I would still have to argue, that the other drives listed by them – such as hunger, fear, sexuality – can be considered as the 'motives' of war at least to the same extent as the so-called 'aggressivity'. All we can say about aggressivity proper is that it may be the 'fuel' for war, but not that it is the motive or incentive for it. But even this 'fuel' is not indispensable, what more, the more developed the technical level on which war is waged, the less this fuel is needed. The soldier preparing for a bayonet attact may still have 'needed' the irritation of rage

[64] Of course, the theory of instincts is merely the starting point and not the adequate territory of the problem of the 'possibility of building-in' with regard to the phenomena analysed below. The many-sided examination of the issue can only take place within the context of the theory of affects and of needs.

or to become inebriated with the notion of 'liberty', but the bomber pilot has not the least need for this, on the contrary, it is only with a cool head that he can calculate the most appropriate moment for releasing his freight of bombs.

It is reasonable to assume that aggressive drive has never brought about war, at least not of itself, and has never even been sufficient 'fuel' for war. Inclination and habit have always been part of this fuel. (I do not speak about projection because the theory of drives considers this the rationalization of the instincts of aggression.) If, on the other hand, the aggressive drive cannot be considered the motive or the cause of war, and even insofar as a contributory factor, it is but one aspect of war, then the institution of war as manifested in history up to the present and as species-specific (insofar as we accept this notion at all) is no proof of the existence of the instinct of aggression.

Let us reach once again into the bag and let us pick out other 'decisive' proofs. Since I have analyzed war in some detail, I will not bore the readers with an analysis of other institutions that are supposed to be outlets for the 'pressure of aggression': such as belief in withcraft, cannibalism, institutionalized revenge, institutionalized races, systems of prejudices characteristic of groups, etc. Everyone may carry out his analysis for himself and will undoubtedly find that the specific causes of these institutionalized 'types of aggression' are heterogeneous, what more, they even differ from case to case, and that 'drive' is but one factor as fuel of action. Nor will I analyse the physical 'affronts' aimed at the destruction or humiliation of other human beings, for instance, the most varied forms of killing, beating and physical brutality the bio-psychological motive of which is (as at least one of the motives) anger, since I have already talked about anger; or habit, rational deliberation or value commitment  – the latter do not belong among the themes of the analysis of the 'instinct of aggression' and merely prove that the totality of actions named by them can in no way be ascribed to some 'instinct of aggression'. I would rather select three entities about which I have not spoken before and which always play a role in the store of facts regarding the evidence of the existence of the instinct of aggression. The entities I have selected are: sadism, hatred, and envy. Even here I have strived to select heterogeneous facts. Sadism is a neurotic-destructive attitude aimed against the other as object and which pervades the entire personality. Hatred is a feeling. Envy is a character trait. The latter two by no means necessarily pervade the entire personality, and hatred may be directed at other than human beings.[65]

---

[65] In the next chapter I will return to the analysis of the connection between frustration and aggression. I only wish to point out here that the phenomenon described is not relevant to this connection, even if there are points of contact.

I must add two qualifications: first of all, I must abstain from analysing all those facts which may be interpreted more or less as analogies to the aforementioned 'typical' examples: thus jealousy, the desire for power, glee at the misfortune of others, ruthlessness, ill-will, etc. I leave the analogical interpretation up to the reader. Furthermore, in my analysis I will keep strictly to the subject of this treatise. Thus I will discuss hatred and envy in much greater detail, from a number of aspects, in my theory of affects.

It is a matter of course that sadism may not be derived exclusively from the aggressive drive; long ago Freud, the most thorough researcher of this theme, has demonstrated that the 'libido' is at least as much a motive of sadism. If we abstain from a direct identification of 'libido' with sexuality, something that is not characteristic of Freud himself, then we must accept this explanation as an incontrovertible fact. Sadism is distinguished from all other forms of destruction aimed against man by the fact that it procures pleasure, causes enjoyment. The release of rage may well result in a release of tension, but not in sensual enjoyment. If we bang our fist on the table this gesture does not imply enjoyment on our part; and if we strike somebody out of rage, this act does not cause pleasure. Or rather, insofar as it also causes pleasure (and this is only possible in the latter case), sadism already plays a part in the gesture. Since rage is not enjoyment and, at the same time, it is a compulsive force at the time of the appearance of the given stimulus, it cannot be planned and cannot be retarded. By dint of will-power it may be possible to diminish the duration of the fit of rage, but it may not be increased (for then it would become manipulated). On the contrary, the act of sadism can be well planned, may well be delayed, extended, what more, intentionality and purposefulness are essentially part of it. It will suffice to think of the discoverer of the phenomenon, of *Justine* of the Marquis of Sade. The sexual sadists in the novel have planned with gothic fantasy the 'situations' in which the victims of their sadism are most apt to be humiliated. There is rage among animals, even if the stimuli provoking it form but a small percentage of the stimuli that provoke human anger, but there is no sadism among animals. The capacity for purposeful action is an intrinsic part of sadism, as is planning and, what is perhaps even more important, so is the perverted relationship between subject and object.

In the majority of cases the sadist subject is not 'enraged' against his object. But this object can only be a subject-object. No one can be sadist with regard to a mere object (against a chair, an institution, or the hail). The pleasure of the sadist is derived from the fact that by his act he is proving the power of his own subject: the power of turning another subject into a mere object. Only a subject can be turned into an object. What more, the main source of pleasure of the sadist is that, in the process of becoming an object, the ever more humiliated, more trampled subject always 'manifests' his own subjectivity. A former prisoner at Auschwitz told about a Lithuanian member of the SS that before shooting to death woman prisoners picked at random he would always shout at them: 'weinen!'. He only derived pleasure from shooting the woman to death if she cried, and begged for her life, if he was able to convert the subject into mere object. The desire of the sadist is not simply to destroy the other, but rather to torture or destroy on the basis of an imagined 'libretto'. This is a perverted form of playfulness: the other person has to perform the rites of the conversion from subject to object. All this, of course, is valid not only in case of the physical destruction of the other, but also for sadism that destroys its spiritual and moral subject, the so-called 'intellectual sadism'. The other is made into an object by being changed into mere instrument, an instrument about which we know (or, in a primitive case, we suspect) that by its essence he should be a goal.

Therefore it would be absurd to talk about sadism as a manifestation of some kind of 'instinct'. It is not related to the only biological constituent of aggression, namely to anger. It may be compulsive in the case of certain individuals (but then it is a psychic phenomenon), as in the case of those who kill in the course of some sexual act, but it is not compulsive in most cases. Sadist personalities are psychic cases, but in the case of non-sadist personalities rational and moral motivation may always prevent the realization of sadist impulses, whereas these motivations are not capable of preventing anger (it is not rage itself that can be regulated, but the coordination of movements that constitutes an outlet for rage: striking somebody, or smashing the cup to the ground). Yet it is not a species-specific phenomenon: among the majority of 'primitive' peoples we never meet with sadism, as far as action is concerned, and it is only among a small minority of modern men that we meet with sadism realized in behaviour or action. Yet rational and moral factors may considerably codetermine sadist action and behaviour in general. To refer once again to the Marquis of Sade, they were the conscious 'apostles' of the principle of pleasure and egotism.

Yet we cannot deny that, at least in the present age, more or less sadist impulses may be detected in a large percentage of individuals. This undeniable fact, however, cannot be accounted for by any theory of instincts. It cannot be explained by the theory of 'instinct of aggression' (as already mentioned), nor even by the instinct to procure pleasure. (In his earlier theory of sadism Freud ascribed this libido to the energies of love and pleasure.) Presumably I need not waste words on how the 'instinct of procuring pleasure' is incompatible with my ideas. All realization of our goals, all development of our capacities, including the capacity to think and to perceive, furthermore a number of stimuli that affect these processes (and connected with our whole personality or some of its aspects) may become the source of pleasure for us. The question is not whether the drive of the procurement of pleasure instigates sadism, but rather why do some derive pleasure from turning other subjects into objects?

The genius of Freud also can be seen in his detection, even if concealed by his theory of instincts, of the affinity between the weakness of the ego and sadism. The ego squirming between the superego of social prescriptions and systems of norms and the *id* that cannot be rationalized, the *id* of repressed impulses and desires (the apt phenomenology of the alienated subject), indeed shows a tendency to sadism. The consciousness of identity with its own self and self-assurance that finds vindication in actions are the basic needs of personality. The weaker the ego, the less it can identify with its own self, the less self-assurance finds strength in sensible actions, the more the need for self-identity appears in a perverted form. If the strength and power of the subject cannot be increased in the realization of its capacities, if the formation of the identity of the subject is hampered by the systems of social norms and institutions or, as in ideological cases, the subject consciously relinquishes the 'channel' partially controlled by the system of norms, of development of his power, then the power of the subject may still grow relatively speaking: by the trampling of the subject of the other, by making the other into an object. If the ego is mere means, it still has two roads of advance, albeit not always equally open: to achieve to become self-goal, at least for *some* others, or to degrade others into more or less means.

To what extent the inclination for sadism (which is not always actual sadism) is a sign of the weakness of the ego – if I may abstract from its ideological forms – can be shown by the example of childhood sadism, which one can obviously outgrow. Gottfried Keller describes such a 'case study' in his short story 'The Village Romeo and Juliet'. In their childhood the two protagonists clearly found sadistic pleasure in the torture of insects. Later on, as their personality was formed, and because of the fact that through their love they became a goal for one another, this sadistic tendency disappeared without leaving a trace. But to speak of ordinary case studies rather than of extreme cases of sadism, can we wonder that the wife subjected to the husband finds pleasure in 'harassing' or 'henpecking' her 'lord' in the strict sense of the word, or that the person humiliated in his love (I do not mean that his love is simply unrequited) will feature the person who has humiliated him ugly and decrepit in his fantasies? Let there be no mistake: I do not mean to absolve these everyday forms of sadism, I merely want to point to the very rational causes for its being so current.[66]

[66] The environmentalist theories, as we shall see, interpret not only the source of hatred in a different manner, but also its object. Thus, according to the group-theory, the source of hatred is the very existence of groups: and the object of hatred is always the 'out-group', or the representative of the out-group.

I don't know if the inclination for sadism is innate or not, whether a lesser or greater quantity of sadism is coded in our genes. But even if it is innate, this does not indicate in any way whether or not we will indeed become sadists, since an infinite quantity of aptitudes and tendencies are coded into us — perhaps in greater or lesser quantities, which never become realized or fall into disuse for lack of an appropriate situation. The existence and currency of sadism is not the social evidence of the instinct or drive of aggression, but rather a sad symptom of the alienation of society as well as of the alienation of the ego from the self.

Of the series of feelings which have served as proof of the instinct of aggression I have picked hatred because it plays such a central role in all interpretations. The book of Eibl-Eibesfeld about the instinct of aggression bears the title *Love and Hate*. The Freudian impact on the theory of aggression becomes evident from the fact that the identification of the object of hatred and the object of love occurs so frequently. Let us recall the statement by Lorenz: 'one can really only hate where one has loved'. Whereas Mitscherlich writes: 'The tendency becomes delayed due to the fact that the repressed libidinal expectations mobilize aggression without actually creating more than substitute feeling or substitute action. It is not satisfied by hatred.'[67] This quotation presents concisely the gist of the argument. According to this argument a) hatred refers to the object of the libido — the person we love, have loved, or wish to love — since the libido cannot 'live itself out'; b) hatred and aggression are synonymous concepts, since hatred is precisely aggression; c) hatred is not a value, since it does not satisfy.

Let us examine these three statements.

The notion that 'one can really only hate where one has loved' has already been questioned. Let me just refer to the type of hatred analyzed in depth by the advocates of the group theory, a type of hatred that has become particularly destructive in our century: hatred directed against the out-group (hatred of Blacks, anti-semitism, etc.), which cannot at all be interpreted as a (form of) manifestation of love. As always the advocates of the drive theory, have, of course, found an explanation for this phenomenon: they speak of projection. We actually hate our father or our lover, but we 'project' this hatred onto the representatives of other nations or ethnic groups, representatives we do not even know personally. In my theory of affects I will endeavour to show in detail that this argument does not stand water. Let it suffice, for the time being, to refer to one of the most important categories of Allport: the category of the so-called 'functional independence'. Allport's line of thought goes as follows: even if we

[67] Alexander Mitscherlich, *Die Idee des Friedens und die menschliche Aggressivität,* Frankfurt: Suhrkamp, 1969, 71.

assume that the ultimate source of hatred entertained with regard to members of an out-group is the hatred against the beloved object, still the former cannot be derived from the latter. For the question is not why we project, but rather why do we project precisely on the members of the out-group. (Why not onto our own group, our own nation, our own ethnic origins, etc.) Whatever the genesis of a feeling or type of activity, its specific forms are always functionally independent, and the only rational interpretation is the analysis of this specific independent function. Particularly when in every instance of the specific functioning of the feeling or type of action certain factors play a part together, and play a part which had no role in the 'genesis', but which belong organically to the feeling or type of action, and which belong organically to the feeling or type of action, and which form a unit with these. The analysis of origins does not explain, but takes apart the totality of the phenomenon to be analysed: rather than say much, the study of the genesis says nothing.

Are the concepts hatred and agression synonymous?

Let us think of the sole biological codeterminant of aggression, that is rage. To begin with, I refer back to my analysis of the circumstances under which we are inclined to say: 'I acted out of rage.' As we have seen, we do this only if the action contradicts our values, if we are not able to justify it *a posteriori*, to rationalize it, or approve of it. If we should strike someone out of hatred, most of the time we would not say 'I struck him out of rage.', but rather, 'I struck him because I hate him.'; we would only refer to rage if we condemn the 'solution' of conflicts by means of physical brutality. If I should intentionally push someone who has jostled me on the city bus, then I have undoubtedly acted out of rage, but can I really say that I hate the person I have pushed? In general I cannot, for I do not even know him. I will interpret my own action as motivated by hatred only if the offender belongs to a group towards which my hatred has formed previously (if I classify the offender into the hated group). Thus, 'I have been jostled by that dirty nigger.', or 'I have been jostled by that suave gentleman.', or 'I have been jostled by that filthy bum.', etc. Thus at most I can say: someone I hate (in his person or his group) will more easily stimulate me to rage than somebody I do not hate – the first is more likely to fill the role of stimulus. Or: I can more easily rationalize my gesture of rage by the communication of a hatred that already exists.

Rage is always of relatively short duration, the 'state of excitation' of the organism describes a rapidly declining curve. Hatred has no 'curve' determined in time. No permanent 'state of excitation' pertains to it, the biochemical processes and the physiological 'symptoms' typical of rage do not characterize hatred. Yet the mention of the object of hatred, especially if positively mentioned, may bring about symptoms similar to, albeit not as intensive as rage, whereas information about some misfortune affecting that object may arouse completely different feelings such as glee or even satisfaction. If we seek the source of hatred in the drive 'given' in the organism, I can say no more than what I have said: in general human beings are strongly impulsive (precisely as a result of the 'hiatus' and, perhaps, because in his prehistory impulsiveness had a positive selective value), but this 'affective content' is not specific, not only from the aspect of the coordination of movement elicited, but even from the social emotional aspect. If man is capable of hating strongly, it is only because he is capable of feeling strongly, of loving strongly, of feeling enthusiasm, of feeling very happy or very sad, of enjoying and desiring strongly, of feeling inebriated with happiness or despondent with pain.

Hatred undoubtedly has a drive function, and this is the circumstance which the advocates of the drive theory have isolated from its other functions. This drive function signifies that hatred may be the cause of my action, but it may not be the purpose of my action, as happiness or enjoyment in their most varied forms and contents may well be. People cannot strive to hate, just as − apart from a few exceptions − they cannot have as their purpose to fear or be hungry. Yet the types of action motivated by hatred are indeed of the kind usually classed under the heading 'aggressivity': the annihilation or harming of others, or at least fantasies regarding such actions.

But even if hatred cannot be one's purpose, it may serve purpose; if it motivates to actions too which are usually described as 'aggression' this does not mean for all that the source of its social function is aggression, even less that the source is some kind of 'instinct of aggression'.

Allow me to repeat briefly what I have already sketched in my book on everyday life: the social function of the pair of affects love-hatred resides in the fact that they are orienting affects. Without the 'yes-feeling' or 'no-feeling' with reference to persons (or groups) we would be unable to orient ourselves in our human relations. Not a single human group would have been able to preserve itself to this day (and precisely because human beings do not have instincts) had it not developed these orientational feelings, and had they not been handed down from generation to generation. 'You may trust in these and these', or 'you must be beware of these and these': society could not function without these and similar precepts and the individual too would perish without their acquisition and application. Social integrations 'assign' to individuals the objects of their love and hatred as traditions and norms. The Christian advice to 'love your enemy' is very modern − in relation to the whole history of mankind − and it exists only as an abstract norm; it has never worked as a specific norm and can never work. The realist perspective for a humane future is not the man who loves his enemies, but the man who has no enemies. Hatred can only cease as an orientational affect when and where it no longer has a social function, and is not handed down as heritage. And, of course, only if the particularist man, the man who spontaneously identifies with his ego-consciousness and his we-consciousness when meeting the other or others, will no longer be socially typical.

The latter is particularly important: hatred can only be directed against inherited objects because human beings, or at least the majority, have an affinity for hatred. The complete identification of the particularist behaviour with its own particularist ego is the anthropological basis of this affinity. If I identify completely with my particularism, then I cannot identify with other, then I respond with hatred to every actual or imagined offence that affects the particularist ego. The inherited object projects the particularist affect on the we-consciousness (as opposed to 'they').

In *Man for Himself* Fromm argues that we must differentiate between 'rational' and 'irrational' hatred. But this notion itself is too 'rational' to be theoretically explicable. If Fromm means to establish as norm that we should hate those about whom we know they are harmful to humanity (for instance, Hitler), and that we should not hate those about whom we cannot demonstrate this (for instance the Jews), then I agree with this as norm. This statement, or norm, endows humanist orientation with value (with regard to affects), but it is not at all by its 'rationality' that it outdoes previous orientations. All hatred that orients is 'rational', and at the same time all hatred is 'irrational' since hatred itself is not a cognitive process, even if it is preceded or accompanied by such processes. Even if by 'irrational' hatred I mean an affect directed against some kind of norm accepted by us, the expression would not be correct. For it is not the feeling that was 'irrational', we only erred in determining or judging its object (this is cognitive error).

Thus we have reached the analysis of the third problem I had selected: can we consider hatred as a 'non-value', inasmuch as it does not satisfy?

Here we must distinguish between the social and historical function of hatred on the one hand, and the role it plays in the development of personality on on the other.

As far as the social and historical aspect is concerned: we cannot regard hatred as either value or non-value (*Wert-Unwert*) because, as we have seen, it is not a value orientational category (just as we cannot consider love as value or non-value).

The situation is different if we analyze hatred from the point of view of development of personality. Here I must point out, however, that I do this on the basis of a previous choice of values. I consider the harmonically developed individual as a value. I consider individual[68] as a value (the

---

[68] I use the term 'individual' in a special sense differing from its meaning in daily usage. Its content is summed up in my *Everyday Life*. To put it roughly: it is the opposite of the particularist person, a member of humankind who has a conscious relation to the species.

distanced relationship to the particularist ego of the individual and, at the same time, to its integration), and I consider the sane (not neurotic) personality as a value. (All this is not some theoretical necessity, nor even some kind of 'rationality' as opposed to 'irrationality', but indeed a personal choice which, of course, is not simply subjective, since it expresses contemporary tendencies, endeavours, needs and abstract norms.) If we consider all these as values then, and only then, do we have the right to consider hatred, as one type of orientational affect, and as opposed to antipathy, as non-value. For, indeed, man cannot develop harmonically, cannot become a sane individual if hatred plays a significant role in his affective orientation (a hatred that does not satisfy and that is aimed at the annihilation of others): in other words, if he is motivated by hatred. Thus the concept of 'irrational' hatred makes sense only if we discuss it not 'ontologically' but with a value accent. For the construction of an emotionally rational personality it is necessary to demolish hatred as an orientational feeling. Such a 'demolition' cannot take place suddenly, by means of some kind of mutation, by forming human beings incapable of hatred. Nor would such a thing be desirable for hatred must indeed exist, and must orient, as long as there are matters 'worthy of hatred'. The so-called 'rational' hatred would be none other than the demolition of inherited customs and norms with regard to the 'selection' of the object of hatred. It would be none other than the selection of the object of hatred based on individual judgment from the following point of view, and only from that point of view: to what extent does somebody prevent, not by his mere existence, but by his actions or behaviour the realization of those values which we have selected for ourselves and which we deem valuable in terms of the future development of mankind. In this case, however, it is no longer hatred that motivates.

I have said that we get a different picture of the value or non-value character ascribed to hatred if we observe its social and historical function, than if we examine the role it fulfills in the development of personality. Undoubtedly, this difference is relative. If we should imagine a society which generally allows for the formation of a harmonically developed, sane personality, then we have said, by the same token, that we are thinking of a society in which hatred no longer has the function of a basic orientational feeling.

Just as hatred cannot be derived from the instinct of aggression, nor is a proof of the existence of that instinct, the same applies to envy. The author of the most comprehensive modern work on envy (Helmuth Schoeck, *Der Neid*, Freiburg: Karl Alber 1968), attempted to demonstrate that it is species-specific, and impossible to eliminate. While Schoeck is not a believer in the drive-instinct theory, or at least he does not consider envy a form of manifestation of the 'instinct of aggression' as those believers do,

61

nevertheless he considers envy an aggressive attitude that has compulsive force. For according to him, compulsive comparison with other human beings pertains to the essence of man. And the stimulus for this sort of comparison is the inequality of man. Since complete equality is impossible, envy, as an aggressive attitude, has always been characteristic of humanity (and of each individual), and will always remain so.

It was already known to Aristotle that the source of envy is comparison. He also knew that we are not envious of persons we do not know and are quite different from us (either as to their position, their wealth, their aptitudes, their age, etc.) The object of envy is not the person who is vastly different, but the similar one. In economics qualitatively different factors may be compared quantitatively, but for envy the condition of comparison is the identity or similarity of quality. Of course, a poet may feel envious of the popularity acquired by an actor, but then it is not his talent as actor that the poet envies, but a common 'qualification': popularity itself, of which the share of the poet is less than that of the actor.

Within the similarity of quality, however, the object of envy is always some kind of quantity (greater wealth, more beauty, more recognition, more success, more luck). This is indicated by the reaction to envy, the method of 'defending oneself' against envy, against aggressions stemming from envy; modesty as self-depreciation. The open manifestation of pride in success, in accomplishment is *hybris*, inasmuch as it stimulates envy. 'It is not my merit.', or 'I was merely lucky.', 'Without your help I could never have managed.', or 'Anyone could have done the same.', such are the formulas, in the majority of cases, which preempt, prevent, or try to prevent aggression stemming from envy.

It is undeniable that the majority of persons indeed react in an aggressive manner to inequality when this inequality is manifested in identical or similar qualities. Nor can it be denied that the cessation of gross social inequalities will not change the matter in the least: for people, as mentioned, do not envy what is far removed, but rather what lies close at hand. The conclusion Schoeck derives from this is that social levelling would increase the quantity of aggression inherent in envy. Nor does the multiplication of contacts diminish envy for, as we know, we are more liable to feel envy towards persons we know than towards strangers.

The question remains, does it follow that aggression stemming from envy cannot be eliminated? To answer this question, we must ask another: is there a value that does not eliminate, but rather presupposes the inequality of man – and I do not mean social inequality – which is identical in quality yet theoretically incommensurable in quantity, and with regard to which comparison is not only not compulsive, but is simply not possible?

There is such a value, and that value is personality.

If X should say 'I would like to be as beautiful as Y.', then he does not at all mean 'I would like to be Y.', but simply that I, while remaining X, would like to acquire an attribute of Y, namely his or her beauty. Even the unformed or the alienated personality does not wish to exchange his or her personality.

For a moment, however, let us imagine a society in which every personality is capable of developing his own capacities in many directions and in which personality has become the main value – and at least I can conceive such a society – then we have by the same token conceived a society in which there is no envy having compulsive strength, since there remains nothing to be envied. What I can make out of myself is theoretically not comparable with what other persons may make out of themselves, inasmuch as there is no quantity which could become a common denominator. If it is precisely our inequality, our being as we are in its totality, as a structure that cannot be decomposed into its 'parts' that becomes the greatest value for us, then we differ from one another, but this difference becomes pure quality. The 'complete man', to quote Goethe, cannot envy another 'complete man', because he is equally complete no matter how different.

Our ability to imagine a society in which there is no envy having compulsive strength is only relevant from a purely theoretical point of view, at least in the present historical period. It only serves to support the view that the emotional and psychological factor of aggression stemming from envy is not necessarily species-specific: this type of aggression is so general because the subject of the unequal society is the alienated personality. Since, however, it seems impossible that every form of social inequality should cease within the foreseeable future (and, at the same time, that all forms of equality should cease), it seems also impossible to eliminate all forms of quantitative comparison between persons; I would be a utopist if I counted on the disappearance of envy, as an emotional-psychological factor, as a reality. The most optimistic possibility with which one may count, and even here, not in the immediate future, and for which at best it may be possible to open the way in social practice, is the development of community norms which, on the average, would prevent the manifestation of aggressive envy in action and which, furthermore, would increasingly raise personality to the level of self-value: in other words, they diminish, in a parallel way, the intensity of the psychological-emotional content of envy.

Among the social proofs of the instinct of aggression I have so far examined an institution (war), a type of aggressive behaviour (sadism), an orientational feeling (hatred), and a character trait having emotional content (envy). All these were merely examples I 'picked out' and on the analogy of which the reader may repeat the analysis with regard to further examples of the sort. But let me repeat, I did not attempt a complex analysis of any of these factors; I have merely referred to certain of their aspects which are decisive with regard to our topic.

Now, to finish, I would like to discuss the 'trumpcard' of the theory of drive-aggression that seems to crop up time and again. This trumpcard is: we do not know of a single culture in which aggression does not play a key role.

Whiting and Child have compared fifty-two cultures (mostly 'primitive' cultures) with regard to the socialization of child behaviour.[69] (This socialization includes training for cleanliness, sexuality, the formation of independence, the sublimation of aggression.) From all this they arrived at the following conclusion: 'Aggression is the system of behaviour with the lowest average degree of indulgence.'[70] Aggression is actually the only behaviour which is 'socialized' strongly and early in every culture (and these two, as Whiting and Child demonstrate – do not go necessarily together at all.) There are cultures where sexual regulation comes very late, but then it is very strict, whereas in certain other cultures it may come early, but remains very 'liberal', etc. The 'types' of socialization vary greatly, of course. In some cultures aggressive attitudes towards adults are strictly prohibited, but are allowed among children (the Kwoma). There are cultures, such as the Arapes, where a method for the general 'release' of aggression has evolved. Here fighting children are separated and kept apart. The separated child is then allowed to stamp his feet, to scream, or to roll in the dust, but he is allowed to return to the community of children only once his fit of rage has passed – and he is not allowed to touch his companion.

All this, per se, rather supports the existence of an instinct of aggression. The reason for the early and strict regulation of aggression in every culture may be precisely the strength of the instinct of aggression. Yet the data presented by Whiting and Child also draw our attention to another factor: that the 'quantum' of aggression for which society must provide an outlet is far from being the same in every 'primitive' tribe. What more, a clear correlation can be shown between the degree of dependency of the child and the 'quantum' of his aggression. I believe this result is not surprising. In the course of my analysis of sadism I have already referred to childhood sadism 'outgrown' by the adult, and to the fact that one of its sources is the weakness of the ego. It seems probable, and the fifty-two cultures used as

[69] One purpose of this work is to refute neo-Freudian environmentalism from the point of view of behaviourism. I will analyse this work later in my book. Let us, for the time being, disregard the ideological preference of the authors, because the body of data supporting their analysis is quite rich and at least relatively independent of the consequences drawn from it.

[70] J. W. M. Whiting and I. L. Child, *Child Training and Personality*, New Haven – London: Yale University Press, 1964, p. 114, 4. Ed.

examples support this interpretation that, although childhood aggression (which, of course, is not the same as childhood sadism) is a social phenomenon, it may be diminished, but cannot be eliminated altogether. I cannot imagine a society in which the child would not require dependency in the course of his socialization in one form or another. No matter how permissive the form of upbringing it cannot allow the child to jump out of the window from the twenty-fifth floor whenever he feels like; this has to be forbidden by resorting to 'authority'. Uniqueness that cannot be quantitatively compared, that is personality, and intention directed at personality as supreme value cannot be 'ready' in the child. The question, therefore, is not whether childhood aggression can be eliminated or not, but whether the aggressive reactions that aim to convert other human beings into means or objects can or cannot be eliminated in the course of the process of socialization.

If we ask the question in this manner, then even a study of 'primitive' tribes may lead to positive conclusions. For no one denies that there are quite a few 'primitive' tribes and groups which know nothing of the aggressive forms of behaviour and reactions aiming at converting other humans into means or objects (for instance the Zuni).[71] But according to the theory of aggressive instinct this circumstance has nothing to do with the existence of a 'quantum' of aggressive instinct. Thus among the Ifalu it is aggression against the spirits that offers an outlet to the quantum of aggressive instinct, whereas among the Zuni it is the cruel initiation rites.[72] Let us for a moment set aside the fact – easy to demonstrate on the basis of data presented by significant anthropologists like Malinowski, Mead and Benedict – according to which the drive-quantum varies greatly from tribe to tribe and, furthermore, the equally well demonstrated fact, that the allowance of the act of aggression, nay, its description in heroic colours is itself a spur to the drive of aggression, and let us turn our attention merely to the 'formal' aspect of the phenomenon. If aggressivity can, for example, only find an outlet in the attitude displayed during the initiation rites of the Zuni, and is capable of being released successfully and a hundred percent in this attitude then we may well say that aggressive behaviour, insofar as social relations are concerned, plays no role whatsoever. If this same aggression in the case of the Zunis manifests itself strictly in the severity of the initiation rites (the social function of which is to try out the capacity of the youth to withstand turning into man), then we are justified in claiming that aggression has no role to play in their social

---

[71] S. Ruth Benedict, *Patterns of Culture*, The Riverside Press, Cambridge, Boston and New York, 1934, pp. 57-125.
[72] S. *op. cit.* p. 69.

existence. Thus H. Helmuth is perfectly justified in speaking of the lack of aggressive behaviour in the case of these 'primitive' peoples.[73]

Thus, even if the conditionality of 'aggressivity' observable among 'primitive' peoples is not yet evidence against the theory of the instinct of aggression, it is nevertheless admissible to assert that the presence of one type of behaviour or another classified as 'aggressivity' is by no means proof of the existence of the aggressive drive.

I have examined the theory of the instinct of aggression from three aspects. I have analysed the theories regarding the genesis of this alleged instinct, the alleged bio-psychological evidence regarding the existence of the instinct, and finally its alleged social evidence. I have shown about all these alleged proofs, that they do not prove what they are meant to prove, and thus we may draw conclusions regarding the non-existence of the aggressive drive. At the same time I have analysed the ideological function and roots of the theory of the aggressive drive.

But it is not only the drive-instinct theory which claims that aggression (i.e. aggressive behaviour) is characteristic of the species and cannot be eliminated. Some of the tendencies that are in polemical opposition to the theory of instinct have arrived at the same conclusion. The peculiarity of the drive-instinct theory, from this point of view, consists in the fact that it formulates its conception naturalistically and means to discover the motive of aggressivity first of all in the biological constitution of man.

The fact that I have rejected the naturalist explanation of aggression stated at the beginning of this work, from the point of view of the theoretical hypotheses and the facts arranged by them, does not mean that I accept its environmentalist critique. The fact that on the basis of these same hypotheses I have rejected the characterization of forms of behaviour and reactions deemed aggressive also by myself as species-specific and as ineluctable, does not yet mean that I deny the dangerous presence of these forms of behaviour in our social existence, or that I consider their elimination as a simple process. Thus, from the aspect of a clear formulation of my stand, I cannot content myself with a critique of the drive-instinct theory. I must formulate a critique of the critique. I should add that in this critique of the critique 'aggression' continues to remain but an example, albeit a rather characteristic one. Thus, for instance, the behaviourists not only refute the theory of the instinct of aggression, but the theory of instincts in general; and so do the neo-Freudians. Hence the criticism of the critics of the theory of the instinct of aggression is also but a typical example of the criticism of the critics of the drive-instinct theory in general.

[73] Professor Szentagothay has called my attention to the fact that among the recently 'discovered' Tasaday ethnic group in the Philippines aggressive behaviour does not manifest itself in any form.

# III  AGGRESSION AS A GENERAL SOCIAL PHENOMENON OR ENVIRONMENTALISM

a)    Behaviourism is about a fifty-year old offshoot of manipulative social theory. Since then it has grown innumerable branches, and it is hardly possible to call attention even to all the most important ones from our point of view. I will concentrate on those traits which definitely differentiate this trend from all others, that is to say, on those notions contributed by behaviourism which have become part of the scientific common stock.

To begin with the most fruitful (or perhaps I should say the only truly fruitful) one: behaviourists consider behaviour as the only source of information. I too believe that behaviour is the main source of information regarding the individual as social being, even if not the only one (for I do not deny the informational value of introspection). For all that the circumstance that behaviour is the main source of information does not mean that it is final reality. Behaviour is not something that cannot be transcended but, on the one hand, it is the complex of the systems of social requirements, customs, and relations, and, on the other hand, of the psychological processes. Therefore, in our knowledge, we cannot afford to stop at the mere description of behaviour. Starting from behaviour we must continue to explore those psychological processes and feelings which find expression in behaviour, furthermore, to explore the social content and value of the 'stimuli' that elicit these processes and feelings; and finally, to explore the relationship of specific behaviour to the total personality.

The latter is particularly important because, at least in the case of human beings, 'behaviour' that are hermetically separated or independent from others do not exist. At least in its classical phase behaviourism has conceived of the concept of behaviour in a narrow sense, as a specific movement coordination, as attitude. The 'response' to a given stimulus was a specific movement coordination or attitude, the particular type of behaviour could only be understood and studied together with its stimulus. But behaviourism does not deal with how these types of behaviour – as responses to their own stimuli – relate to one another, and how their relationship is constituted in the integral personality of man; in fact, it even considers such an inquiry as 'unscientific'.

Let us recall that there are independent movement coordinations in the case of animals, elicited by specific internal and external stimuli: and this was precisely what I have called instincts. According to the behaviourist interpretation instinct does not exist – or at least cannot become the object of scientific investigation – (nor does internal stimulus exist), but man and animal alike are characterized by movement coordinations or types of reaction that are independent of each other and are elicited by external stimuli. Animal and human organism alike is some kind of mechanism which is conditioned in diverse ways by external stimuli. As Watson writes: 'Man is an animal different from other animals only in the types of behaviour he displays.'[74]

Or let me quote, after the fist behaviourist, the most important representative of the trend living today, and his latest declaration at that. Skinner claims:

> Instinct and drive are fictions-things put inside a person to explain his behaviour. . . If food is reinforcing, it's not because food reduces a drive but because it has been a very good thing for the species that food has reinforced the behaviour of hungry people.[75]

Of course, the almost fifty years that have elapsed have modified the theory. Watson denied the existence of every innate capacity of man, including inherited talent. But in an age that is acquainted with the genetical code, this extremist view proved untenable. Skinner includes in the 'how' of the individual's reaction response the 'genetic fact'. This refinement, however, does not alter a bit the already mentioned functional 'breaking-up' of the personality. If the 'correct' action is rewarded, rather than punished, then people will act correctly and rightly, in response to a given situation, in a given place and to a given stimulus, claims Skinner. As to the criteria for the 'rightness' or 'correctness' of the action, I will discuss Skinner's views further on. For the time being suffice it to make note of the fact of 'breaking-up'. The parent who rewards raises 'correct' children, the plant executive who rewards raises 'correct' workers and clerks, the psychiatrist who rewards raises 'correct' patients.

Reinforcement makes man correct in relation to the accomplishment to which he is spurred by reward.

From the point of view of behaviourist environmentalism categories such as 'human nature', 'human essence', 'species character', (Gattungsmäßigkeit) are irrelevant. Man can be conditioned to everything, without limit in the case of Watson, within the limits determined by genetical facts for Skinner. The latter, however, does not touch upon behaviour. The individual may relearn anything at all with regard to

---

[74] John Watson, *Behaviourism*, The University of Chicago Press, 1959, V.
[75] B. F. Skinner in *Will Success Spoil B. F. Skinner?* by E. Hall, in *Psychology Today*, November 1972.

behaviour, there is nothing in his constitution that resists or could resist the process of 'relearning'. Of course, and here we are dealing with the limits of natural 'propensity', people cannot be retaught to fly by growing wings, nor can everyone be taught to paint like Leonardo. But within these extreme limits human beings can be manipulated to do anything.

Let us recall: it was with sympathy and in agreement I have quoted Kuo who claims that, from the aspect of behaviour, nature is not what can unfold from within, but what can be built in. But now I must raise the opposite question: is nature really so malleable that everything can be built in it, even from the aspect of behaviour? And to apply my question to our own species: can everything be built into human 'nature'?

I will attempt to answer this question later, because it is decisive from our point of view. For the time being let me just call attention to the ideological aspect of behaviourist thought regarding unlimited building-in. First of all: its ideological basis is rationalism carried to its logical conclusion. Human behaviour is clearly and exclusively shaped by learning; in the process of 'trial and error' the 'adequate' behaviour is worked out, that is the behaviour capable of providing a rational response to the given impulse. Humanity, or the transformation of humanity, is synonymous with 'relearning'. The individual who responds to stimuli with rational behaviour is the one who is in working order, and 'being in working order' is the value which the allegedly value-free theory has chosen as its hidden starting point. Of course, in order for the individual mechanism to be in working order the social mechanism must be in working order: to wit a society in which everything is rational and can be rationalized, in which the stimuli themselves are rational goals, and goals that can be attained, at that. Non-rational goals and ones which cannot be attained by mere calculation are what disturb the process of learning and re-learning, the normal functioning of the social and individual mechanisms. Therefore, we need a society, argues Watson 'free of foolish customs and conventions',[76] meaning by foolish everything that cannot be comprised under the category of goal-rationality. The title of Skinner's latest book is *Beyond Freedom and Dignity*; for, according to Skinner, the struggle for freedom and human dignity impedes the elaboration and wide application of a successful behaviourist technique.

I believe all this should suffice to support my initial thesis: behavioursim is the appropriate ideology of sophisticated manipulation. And this is no mere label which I have 'glued' on to the theory, but is in harmony with the admissions of some of the representatives of the theory themselves. Skinner considers it an error that we are too afraid of manipulation. It is true that he rejects the accusation of fascism, adding

[76] John Watson, *Op. cit.,* p. 302.

rightly that fascism manipulates primarily by punishment and not by reinforcement. At the same time he is honest enought to confess: there is no guarantee that fascist regimes would not make use of the behaviourist technique elaborated by him for their own purposes. That his ideal is not this kind of society, but one that is free of conflicts, 'controlled', yet liberal in its forms of life – all this does not detract from the significance of this confession.

Human beings are, in the last analysis, machines, machines for relearning. But to keep machines in working order it is necessary to have someone to guide the machines. Modern machines are guided by science. The responsibility of science is to decide what 'stimuli' should be 'administered' to man and under what conditions, in order to form their adequate response reactions. The scientists and the chief controllers decide, moreover, what behaviour, what reaction may be considered 'correct', on the basis of the category of 'efficiency'. What colour to paint the walls of the plant for the workers to feel 'pleased', how many times hotdogs should be served for the spirit of competition to persist, what machines must be used in schools for the children to give 'adequate' responses, how should the genetical code be modified to give birth to heirs in good 'working order'. 'Science', however, is not an abstract entity, for science is pursued by scientists. Thus, willy-nilly, behaviourism (at least in its classical form[77]) votes for the requirements of a new social hierarchy. On one hand there are the 'scientists', who work out the theories for the adequate stimuli, and give them practical application, or at least: mean to introduce them; whereas on the other hand, we have 'common men', who give the desired 'responses' to these stimuli. *Huxley's Brave New World* is, indeed, the caricature of the behaviourist ideal. It is remarkable that the theory of the absolute possibility for manipulation is willy-nilly put to question precisely by the only consistent behaviourist work which deals with the problem of aggression: by *Frustration and Aggression*, the work of Dollard and his collaborators, which has justly attained world-renown.

In what way is this book consistently behaviourist? First of all because it explains aggression on strictly 'environmentalist' grounds, moreover as response reaction to a given stimulus. This stimulus is frustration. There is no stimulus without response: 'the existence of frustration always leads to some form of aggression'[78] – thus the categorical declaration on the very first page of the book.

A stimulus elicits a response reaction, and it is only between these two

[77] Some disciples of Skinner have come close to the theories of Sears and Laing, that is to the 'third trend'.
[78] J. Dollard and others, *Frustration and Aggression,* London, Kegal Paul, Trench, Trubner & Co., Ltd., 1944, 1.

that there can exist a rationally measurable and examinable connection, which is, as we have seen, also an inevitable connection. The idea that the same frustration may provoke aggression in one personality – as a result of his total personality – whereas it may not provoke aggression in other personalities – still as a result of the organic unity of those personalities – is irrelevant from the behaviourist mode of inquiry. Likewise one may not ask whether the same stimulus may signify frustration for one person, but not for another. For if one does, it would already be a matter of 'evaluation', a matter of the fact that different persons interpret the same stimulus in different ways, from the point of view of their total system of values. Either one of the considerations mentioned above is sufficient to place in jeopardy the mechanistic interpretation of the human organism. Moreover, Dollard and his collaborators have intentionally omitted anger from their analysis, although we have seen how significant a role it plays in the theories of aggression. Human psyche being only a 'black box' it should be 'bracketed', according to Dollard. What can be observed and studied as behaviour is simply one stimulus – one response, one frustration – one aggression.

How do Dollard and his collaborators conceive of frustration? 'Frustration is independently defined as that condition which exists when a goal-response suffers interference.'[79] Hence the whole of the personality cannot be frustrated; the sole origin and process of frustration that can be described, is the blocking of a person's rational goal. What may be the rational goal, what blocks it, who resorts to it and for what reason, all these are matters of 'content' and, as such, irrelevant (a question of appraisal). Frustration is impediment of any of my goals to which I respond with aggression, unconditionally and necessarily.

The interpretation I put in the mouth of the behaviourists 'no matter what the goal may be', is not arbitrary. The examples presented in the book of Dollard imply and emphasize this. The child, who wants to eat an ice-cream, and whose parents will not allow it (either because the child has a cold, or because he is being punished, or because they cannot afford it – from this point of view it doesn't matter) will respond with aggression to this impediment of reaching his goal in the same way as the employee whose boss refuses to grant him a rise (for whatever reason), or the man who is almost killed in battle.

Yet: Dollard and his colleagues not only claim that every frustration brings about aggression, that every frustration is an impediment to the realization of a goal, but also that only frustration may bring about aggression, that aggression can have no other origin.

Before giving a presentation of the critiques of the frustration-

---

[79] Dollard, *Op. cit.*, p. 8.

aggression theory, more precisely, of some of its aspects, I must explain why I consider this book significant in spite of its behaviourist ideology and its one-sidedness. First of all because I too believe that frustration, though maybe not the only, the exclusive origin of aggression, is nevertheless its most important source; and Dollard's work present certain correlations one can make use of even on the basis of different ideological hypotheses. At the same time, as I have already mentioned, the book's consistent behaviourist approach actually works against the final behaviourist conclusions: for a rationally structured system of stimuli that would not frustrate some persons at all is simply inconceivable – using the term frustration in the sense given to it by Dollard and his colleagues. It is impossible for reasons of principle that a specific goal towards which many strive should be achieved by all. It turns out, therefore, that the rational society imagined by Watson and his disciples elicits an irrational reaction (irrational because not leading towards the goal) precisely because of its pure goal rationality. For it is precisely those values, the 'foolish' prejudices and conventions which Watson deems the sole obstacles along the road leading to the paradise of rationalism, which are the only possible preserves of a process by which man can interpret the blocking of his goals as either 'correct' or 'incorrect', and which is the only condition for the elimination of the 'irrational' reaction, in the sense of the behaviourist interpretation of so-called frustration, i.e. aggression. So it is precisely the analyses of Dollard that reveal the necessary connection between the rationalist 'mechanism' and the irrational 'responses'.

Furthermore, the analyses presented by Dollard became the starting points for important empirical research and pertinent theoretical conclusions which placed the aggression-prompting peculiarities of the 'stimuli' of capitalist society into the focus of attention. Thus the work of Hovland and Sears, which appeared in 1940, demonstrated statistically that the number of lynchings in the southern states in the thirties was inversely proportionate to the rise in the cotton price or, in other words, the lack of material security provided by capitalist economy was significantly related to acts of aggression. Berkowitz, whose work I shall have occasion to mention again, also demonstrated by means of empirical data that frustration and aggression are caused mostly by competition; and not only in the case of those who compete and lose, but also for those who prevail or win out. The sources of aggression are not only defeat, but the very fact of competition and the fear of defeat. Thus only a step remains to reach the conclusion that the elimination of material insecurity and, furthermore, the decrease of the constant disposition to compete that is organically connected to capitalism at every stage (including its most recent stages), would eliminate one of the principal 'impulses' for aggression from the lives of individuals. (The competition-centred attitude is also, incidentally, a form of insecurity; if my self-justification can only be victory in competition then my existence is insecure due to the fact that I may become a loser, even if 'defeat' in no way implies financial bankruptcy.)

I will mention only those critics of the theory of Dollard and his companions who did not elaborate another coherent theory to replace behaviourism, but questioned its premises on the grounds of empirical research. Thus Jones, Hester, Farina, and Davos arrived at the following conclusion in the course of a series of experiments conducted in 1959: not every frustration provokes aggression, and not every blocking of goals is regarded by people as frustration. The same individuals may react differently to the same 'frustration' depending on from whom it originates (do they like him, do they trust, is he an authority figure to them, what is the source of this authority, etc.) Furthermore, their reaction varies according to whether or not they know the cause of the 'act of frustration', whether they consider this cause sensible or senseless, or on how they evaluate the cause as motive. Different people react differently to the same frustration, depending on their individuality, on their values, on the strength of their self-confidence, etc. The last aspect, namely self-confidence and self-evaluation, will play a special role in the criticism of the behaviourist school presented by the 'third school', or in its theory of frustration (see White and Lippit). Others, primarily Erikson and his school, rightly reproach Dollard and his companions of having neglected a very important aspect: the frustration tolerance. The individual does not respond to every frustration, even if evaluated and understood as such, with aggression, because a certain 'frustration tolerance' has developed in him; he 'tolerates' certain types of frustration, these represent 'stimuli' against which he does not have reaction responses at all. Let me add: the frustration tolerance is indeed a psychological attitude necessary to the development of every personality. Although it may be exceptional to 'offer the other cheek', it is not only morally required, but also a sign of spiritual sanity to develop indifference with regard to certain frustration. The person who is never able to say, 'What do I care what people say about me!', who can never bear with indifference an ostensibly unfair mark or grade, or cannot tolerate to be unjustly kept in the background as opposed to someone less deserving, will never become a spiritually healthy person. And even if the frustration tolerance must have its limits, to relinquish tolerance does not necessarily mean aggression. It may result in the most varied types of reaction, depending on the whole of the personality. For instance, it may result in shunning the frustrating person or situation, the choice of a new situation, an attempt to realize our blocked goals along a different road, etc. But what is most important, in my opinion, and which is not taken into account either by the Dollard theory, or by the frustration-tolerance theory, is the reaction of one person to the frustration suffered by another.

Here I must refer once again to what I have said about the 'bag' containing heterogeneous behaviour and reaction types lumped together. For behaviourism collects its heterogeneous elements in the selfsame bag as the theory of drives, it only interprets the origins of the forms of behaviour collected in the bag in a different manner. As proof of the connection between frustration and aggression Berkowitz is equally liable to cite the tantrums of children deprived of their ice-cream directed against the parents or the fact that the victims of the London airraids blamed their sufferings on the lack of precautions taken by their government. Only he forgets to point out that the child had been deprived of his own ice-cream, whereas the government was blamed even by those who did not suffer at all in the airraids, who rebelled because these airraids cost the lives of 'others'. Have Dollard and his companions never heard of children who rebelled against their teacher because of injustice suffered not by themselves, but by others? Have they never heard of those Russian 'nihilists' who became enemies of the tsarist regime because they witnessed how their aristocratic parents humiliated the servants day by day? 'Aggression and antagonism are synonymous terms.'[80], claims Dollard. Of course, what I have already demonstrated in connection with the drive-instinct theory is also applicable to this theory: everything in it 'can be reduced' to the basic 'formula'. The event cited above can also be described as follows: the goal of the aristocratic child was to establish friendly relations with the 'servants', but his parents hampered him in this endeavour and thus, finally, he was frustrated in the attainment of his goal, etc. But assuming, without accepting, that this 'deduction' describes the process adequately, we can but refer once again to the functional independence mentioned by Allport. Indignation at the injustice done to others, and the 'antagonism' that stems from it are functionally independent from the response reaction given to the offense against my particularist personality; it simply has a different function with regard to social coexistence, to morality, etc. I must add that, of course, it makes a great deal of difference, both morally and socially, whether a person responds with 'antogonism' to an offense against him and only against him, or whether he interprets the offense done him within a larger context: as a sub-case of all those offenses and injustices which affect a social stratum or class.

It follows from all this that neither of the two interpretations I have described transcends theoretically the interpretation of the individual as

---

[80] It is in this sense that he analyzes (and generalizes for his theory) the conception of class antagonism in *Communist Manifesto*, op. cit. 16-17.

mere particularity. It is not simply a matter of whether the individual responds with aggression to every frustration, or whether he develops within himself that so-called 'frustration tolerance', but also, whether he is capable of perceiving the offense against him within a general context, and to react to this general context, or whether he is capable of responding to the 'frustration' affecting others with the same indignation or even 'antagonism' as he would to the offense against himself. In other words, whether he is capable, in this regard, of crossing from the particularist behaviour to individuality. It is only within this context that it makes sense to ask to what extent and in what situation, etc. is it desirable and to what extent is it not desirable to develop the 'frustration tolerance'. For, as a matter of tendency at least, it would be desirable to develop this faculty when the offense affects merely my particularity, when no kind of distancing from the self can be carried out, when I would be relatively unable to place myself into the point of view of the 'other', furthermore, when the motive of the act causing the offense itself was not particularist, was not meant to cause me harm. On the other hand, it would not be at all desirable when the motivation is itself the offense or, the humiliation, when in spite of the distance from the particularity the act may not be interpreted as justified; furthermore, and this is the most important, when it affects not simply the particularist personality, but affects values, the totality of the individual, in other words, when it affects others along with myself, others whose values and situation I voluntarily share. The former frustration-tolerance is a manifestation of strength of character, the latter of weakness.

The 'weak points' of Dollard's interpretation were noted not only by his ideological adversaries, but even by those who basically accepted the behaviourist theory of aggression. The most significant among the latter was the already mentioned Leonard Berkowitz who, in his work titled *Aggression: A Social Psychological Analysis*, attempts to 'round out' the theory presented by Dollard.

The principal aspect of Berkowitz' contribution is that he adds the category of anger to the theory as a mediating element of the relationship frustration-aggression. Frustration does not elicit aggression directly, but through the intermediary of anger. Certain specific stimuli convert the already existing anger into aggression, 'Anger refers to the emotional state, presumably resulting from frustration, which, in the presence of a suitable cue, instigates responses,'[81] because it makes it possible to interpret projection within the given conception. Aggression is not necessarily directed against the frustrating agent. The drive accumulated in the course of frustration may appear in the form of aggression even against those who

---

[81] Leonard Berkowitz, *Agression: A Social Psychological Analysis*, New York: McGraw-Hill, 1962, p. 1.

did not at all frustrate the affected individual. Thus the stimulation is doubled. There is a starting stimulus – the actual frustration – and a secondary stimulus, which may even be completely accidental or which, in most cases, is one aspect, perhaps a system of norms or channels socially permissible, desirable, or even demanded. What more: without the least hesitation Berkowitz pretends that aggression directed against something other than the frustrating agent is its more typical form. He gives an example I have already quoted, although it does not seem too appropriate: the Germans bombarded London but the victims did not respond primarily by hatred of the Germans, but rather made their own government responsible. (The example is not appropriate because, in my opinion, blaming the government is not aggression and, moreover, it seems quite justified and rational in the given instance.)

What is really significant in Berkowitz' 'contributions', and which once again puts into doubt, willy-nilly, the correctness of the entire basic theory, is the concept of the so-called instrumental aggression he introduces. (In some places Berkowitz refers to the same as 'strategic aggression'.) Berkowitz was able to introduce the category of 'instrumental aggression', which, by the way, is by no means a behaviourist concept, because he acknowledged earlier the intermediary role of 'anger' with regard to frustration-aggression. Thus he had to describe those aggressive acts, and forms of behaviour in which anger plays no role, and the causes of which, therefore, must be sought somewhere else than in frustration in a distinguishing manner since, according to him, frustration always elicits anger. The main examples of instrumental aggression are, according to Berkowitz, war and business competition. Both take place for specific objectives (acquisition of territory, wealth, etc.) which do not stem from frustration of goals, or at least not typically so. Yet in both cases we must speak of aggression, and for two reasons. First of all because the objective of the action is the harming or annihilation of the other party, that is, the objective is identical with that of the aggressive action or of behaviour stemming from frustration. Secondly, because, this kind of goal of the annihilation of others makes it necessary to reorient anger into these channels, that is, to use aggression stemming from frustration as a tool and even to develop it by manipulation. The problem is not whether the initiators or propagators of wars really believe that the enemy has offended their nation or that he is guilty, harmful, worthy of hatred; but in order to achieve their goal they must make the masses they mobilize believe that the reserves of anger stemming from frustration are being released through these channels. Aggression stemming from frustration is the necessary condition of instrumental aggression.

In spite of all these modifications the theory of Berkowitz remains a typical behaviourist environmentalist theory. And since he does not share, in consistent behaviourist style, the notion of frustration tolerance (which, as we have seen, makes sense from a certain aspect), his actual final conclusion does not differ from the end conclusions reached by other behaviourist theories of aggression. Since there is no society, and theoretically there can be none, in which frustration does not exist, in the broad sense of the term, and since it is not possible for human beings to become adults, and co-exist in a society in which the individual never meets frustration in one goal or another, aggression is necessarily part of social existence. Thus the aggression theory of behaviourist environmentalism makes it even less possible than the naturalist instinct-drive theory to imagine a society in which aggression will not be the typical behaviour of individuals.

b) The theory of instrumental aggression is already bordering on another kind of environmentalist theory of aggression, that of the so-called group theory. The premise of the group theory is the undebatable fact that humanity has never been a single unified integration. Individuals are not born into humanity, but into specific integrations. This is their in-group, and all other integrations or groups are out-groups for them. The necessary, always present constituent of the functioning of groups is the we-consciousness: the individual identifies with the group into which he is born. This we-consciousness is a necessary condition for the cohesion of the group, for integration. But this we – consciousness can only be conceived along with a you – consciousness or they – consciousness. We can only be 'we Europeans' if we contrast ourselves to the you-non-Europeans; we can only be 'we Christians', if we contrast ourselves with 'you pagans', or you heretics, etc. Of course, the individual, from the time of a certain period in the evolution of society, gets to chose his own integration in many respects (the we Catholics can become we Protestants, etc.) All this does not alter the fact that social existence is not possible without such particularist integrations, and that the particularist integration cannot function without a we-consciousness, or a they-consciousness. That humanity is necessarily divided into smaller integrations, or is constituted by smaller integrations, presupposes the oppositions of 'familiar' and 'alien', of 'mine' and 'yours'. Identification is separation by the same token. 'Unfamiliarity' itself breeds aggression: we do not trust strangers. An offense by a stranger is immediately interpreted as an offense against our integration. At the same time, the development of aggression against the 'out-group' becomes necessary and inevitable in order to strengthen the cohesion of integration. To resume: according to the interpretation of the group theory the source of aggression is not frustration, but the existence of particularist integrations. According to Sargent every group prescribes aggression towards other groups as a norm, especially towards those groups which in some respect stand in a relationship of rivalry with ours. And here we need not limit ourselves to the basic integrations (nation and neighbouring nation, religious sects fighting for 'souls'), since much simpler and more 'primitive' groups elicit reactions that are quite similar. In the schools class 'a' becomes 'aggressive' towards class 'b' and vice-versa, whereas the fans of one athletic team will show 'aggression' towards the fans of another, etc. The groups cohesion renders so-called 'objective' perception impossible.

There can be no doubt that the group theory has uncovered one of the important sources of aggression. There can be no doubt, furthermore, that we may not presume a humanity, even in the distant future, which would not consist of relations between various integrations. Even those whose principal activity is aimed at the 'species objectivations for themselves' (fürsichseiende gattungsmäßige Objektivationen) take part in some specific integration, even if only in an ideal form; in any case, it is not possible to conceive of a community the we-consciousness of which would function without a they-consciousness. The question is whether, in a future we project, this they-consciousness that forms along with the we-consciousness must necessarily constitute a source of aggression or not?

We must count with three necessary conditions to conceive of such a future. One would be the cessation of the feeling of strangeness, and not of difference, in the relationship between integrations. Another would be: the withering away of the competitive spirit between integrations. The third would be the general transformation of human behaviour from particularist to individual, something that would include – as I have pointed out in my book, *The Everyday Life* – a distanced relationship to our own integration. The experiences of our present age cannot form the basis of much optimism in this regard, for the time being. First of all because the material basis for such a change in behaviour, the integration of human production, has not yet come about. Furthermore, and this is part of the same problem, because even among groups intending the radical transformation of human society the strengthening of group cohesion through hostility against other groups and integrations is no less pronounced than among other integrations of our time. Hence I consider radical tolerance the necessary subjective precondition of a possible future; a tolerance in the framework of which every integration aimed at the 'radically new' would claim to be the embodiment of some particularist need, and at the same time would recognize the right of existence of other kinds of integrations embodying other radical needs, and their legitimacy (relatively speaking). I have selected radical tolerance of that sort as a value. If this value is not realized then the conception of aggression of the group theory remains irrefutable, at least as far as the foreseeable future is concerned.

c) The third and purely environmentalist theory of aggression was elaborated by the neo-freudians. I am referring to those who have un-equivocally rejected the Freudian theory of instincts, including the determining role of the Oedipus complex in the development of person-ality. They have adopted from Freud and placed at the centre of their ideas the decisive role played by the experiences, the traumas, the events of infancy in the whole subsequent development of personality, including the aggressive or non-aggressive bent of the personality. In this environmen-talism the concept of 'environment' becomes extraordinarily narrow, for it actually means nothing more than the family and, within the family, the mother. It is the family and particularly the relationship of the mother to the child that decides, once and for all, whether the child will become aggressive, and to what extent. Erikson writes: '. . . the drives man is born with are not instincts they are'. . . drive fragments to be assembled, given meaning, and organized during a prolonged childhood. . .'[82] The basic character of the person is determined in early childhood, under the in-fluence of parental environment, states Horney in a similar vein.[83]

As a consequence of the narrowing down of the concept of environ-ment, the following factors play a decisive role in the shaping of the personality, as far as the neo-Freudians are concerned: whether the mother cuddless the child or not, does the child partake of her love by means of the 'warmth of her body', does she keep to the hours prescribed for breast-feed-ing, or is the infant fed when he desires (according to Erikson the Dakota Indians are not aggressive because they had been fed whenever they desire). Furthermore, is the child weaned suddenly or gradually (the first become aggressive, since they had had to undergo a trauma, whereas the second are not), are they toilet-trained by force or do the parents wait until cleanliness becomes the child's own requirement, are they being punished for messing themselves, etc. In other words, the satisfaction of the so-called 'oral' and 'anal' needs, or traumas, stemming from such situations are decisive regarding the future of the personality – these are the factors that determine the aggressive or non-aggressive bent of the future person.[84]

If we take neo-freudian environmentalism literally, we may say this one is the most optimistic of the theories of the instinct of aggression, since it is the one that bears to the greatest extent the spirit of Enlightenment. Since, inasmuch as the formation of a non-aggressive humanity is our goal, all we have to do then is to convince the parents by means of psychological and health education that they should hold the infant close to their bodies, that the infants should be breast-fed adjusting to the hunger of the infant,

---

[82] Erik H. Erikson, *Childhood and Society*, Middlesex: Penguin, 1969, p. 89.
[83] S. K. Horney: *Our Inner Conflicts*, London, Kegan Paul, 1946, p. 119 and *passim*.
[84] Ibid.

that they should be weaned gradually at a stage when the infants themselves prefer a more varied diet, that the infants' concern with cleanliness should be the result of the evolution of their own needs, etc. Undoubtedly, there is not a single one of these prescriptions that would be beyond the reach of today's civilized mankind.

I have no reason to deny that the experiences of early childhood indeed play a decisive role in the formation of character, that the parents' attitude towards the child indeed influences extremely, at least on the average, the psychological makeup of growing persons, that the being who grew up in the midst of love and care is himself more capable of loving, that the attitude of trust in particular becomes a significant factor in the decrease of aggressive tendencies. Yet the reduction of environmentalism to early family environment, particularly to the role of the mother, provokes a number of justified objections.

On one hand, even if we consider the narrowest family 'environment', its influence on the infant cannot be limited to the satisfaction of solely oral and anal needs, or to traumas. Every parent is a member of society and conveys not only psycho-hygienic factors but, willy-nilly, his whole social being, attitudes, and thinking to his or her child. To mention only the simplest problem: this kind of social hygiene would make it necessary for the mother not to work, or to work within reach of the child. Whether this criterion can be realized, considering the opportunities available to whole social classes is one question that arises; but it still remains to be seen whether this social hygiene at *this* price would be something desirable? The parent also talks to the child, and thereby communicates his socially 'co-determined' mode of thought, and his ability to express himself. The infant lives not only in the environment of his parent, but in that of other persons as well, such as siblings, neighbours, furthermore in the environment constituted by a variety of objects.

But let us suppose an 'ideal type' in which the psycho-hygienic factors prescribed by the neo-Freudians are all present. In such an environment how would it be possible for that certain frustration-tolerance, which I have found so basic from the point of view of the disappearance of aggressive 'reaction-response', to evolve? If the environment artificially eliminates all frustrations from childhood, then frustration-tolerance cannot evolve, and the development of the personality of the child-ideal posited by the neo-Freudians may head in the direction of two kinds of behaviour. Either he would react with aggression to all manners of frustration (since he never 'became accustomed' to its tolerance), or would not react with so-called 'aggression' to any kind of frustration at all, since all the psychological conditions for resistance have been smothered in him. I believe either type would be disastrous from the point of view of the future of mankind.

All this, however, is but an experiment in thought, since the facts are sufficiently clear. Let us refer, once again, to the study of Whiting and Child. As I have already mentioned: they have compared fifty-two cultures with regard to various 'behaviours'. These behaviours were: suckling and weaning, 'toilet training', the development of independence, the relation to aggression, and sexual freedom or lack of it. The examination bore the following results: there is no kind of correlation between these various types of behaviour respectively, their formation. And what interests us particularly: there is no significant connection between the duration of suckling, the gradual or sudden nature of weaning, the beginning and strictness of anal training on the one hand, and the permissibility or prohibition of aggressivity, of aggressive behaviour on the other hand. Among the inhabitants of the Marquesas – a cannibal tribe – weaning takes place rather early; but it is equally early among the Tanala (maximum six months) which is not at all an aggressive tribe. The Lepcha of India sometimes suckle until the age of puberty, since food is scarce – but for this same reason aggression is plenty. The Manus are not rendered more aggressive by secret masturbation than the Pukapukans among whom the practice of mastrubation is allowed and open.

I reiterate: I do not mean to deny the role of childhood environment on the development of personality (including the formation of aggression). I merely assert the following: the childhood environment cannot be narrowed down to the immediate parental environment, influence cannot be limited to anal, oral, and sexual behaviour, the 'psychohygienic' relationship to the child is ambivalent, its value and influence depends on society in general; last, but not least, the psychological character developed in childhood is not the unconditional and sole determinant of a sub-sequent aggressive or non-aggressive bent. It is true that psychological character develops early; but moral and intellectual character develops considerably later, and may be transformed as well. And since aggression is not simply a psychological phenomenon, since it is not simply identical with the state of rage, since the evaluation, interpretation, intellectual and moral 'elaboration' of the provoking stimuli all pertain to it, I cannot accept, even with regard to aggression, the enlightened determinism of the neo-Freudians.

## IV THE 'THIRD TREND' OF ANTHROPOLOGY OR THE NATURALISM OF THE THEORY OF PERSONALITY

The expression 'third trend' originates with Maslow. The term itself indicates that all those who profess to belong to this trend, or who are classed as belonging to this trend, engage in polemics in two directions at once. On the one hand they criticize the drive-instinct theory, on the other hand they criticize environmentalism. The various representatives of this trend took off from various points to arrive at essentially similar conclusions. Among their basic sources we find Freud, Goethe, Hegel, existentialism and Marx too.

The common 'credo' of the representatives of this 'third trend' is that the total personality is the alpha and omega, the starting point, and the main topic of every kind of anthropology. Human beings have no basic instincts or drives from which the development of the personality can be recreated or derived; nor can this personality be described as the simple mechanism of responses to stimuli that are independent of each other. At the same time, it is not true that everything can be built into man, as behaviourism claims. Human personality can be built in *ad infinitum*, but in one direction only, that is in the direction of human essence, of the species essence (Gattungswesen). As soon as society 'build into' the individual modes of behaviour which contradict the species essence, or the substance of man, the individual ceases to be a wholesome personality and becomes neurotic. If this kind of 'building in' becomes predominant, a 'sick society' comes about. In such cases, we may deal with two alternatives, at least in theory. One alternative would be that the sick society with its sick or neurotic individuals becomes incapable of functioning and collapses, and the individuals unable to communicate in this totally alienated world can no longer fill the task of making society 'work'. The other alternative is that the trampled human substance 'rebels' against the sick society and the alienated 'environment', and creates a 'sane' world to its own measure. I have said, however, that these two alternatives exist only theoretically for the representatives of the 'third trend', because – apart from Marcuse who, in spite of his world-wide influence, has been the only one to draw conclusions that take the first alternative into account – the actual representatives of the trend have considered only the second alternative. For this reason a kind of philosophical utopianism characterizes the representatives of the 'third trend', and this utopianism is the reason why they do not place a question mark, for the most part (not from the point of view of the present, but of the future), next to the realization of the sane society; albeit the question mark can be, nay has to be, added.

I have mentioned that one of the crucial categories for the representatives of the 'third trend' is the human substance, or human essence. Yet they use the concept 'human essence' in a sense different from the one I had proposed at the beginning of this study, in the wake of Marx.[85] The difference does not consist primarily in the way of conceiving of the constituents of the 'species essence' (Gattungswesen): the 'third trend' refers roughly to the same constituents as had Marx. The basic difference lies in the denial of the theoretical possibility of the separation between the species and the individual in disregarding the objectivations, as carriers, mediators, and representatives of the 'species essence', as well as the function of the objectivations as creators of needs. The representatives of the 'third trend', if you like, transform the Marxian thought into a Kantian direction. According to them there are two beings in every man, the *homo noumenon*, which represents the species essence, the actual 'human nature', and the *homo fenomenon*, which is the alienated man reacting to the 'stimuli' of an alienated society; and in every personality there lives the authentic and the inauthentic personality 'together', the 'sane' personality along with the 'sick' personality. The 'true' and 'authentic' nature of man – which lies concealed in every human individual – is identical with the 'sane person', whereas the inauthentic being, which is 'present' in practically every individual of every alienated society, is identical with the 'sick' or 'neurotic' man. Society with its own objectivational systems, requirements, institutions, and systems of norms is either 'favourable' to the development of the sane substance, or allows the 'sick' and 'inauthentic' nature to become predominant, repressing the 'substance' concealed in every man.

The representatives of the 'third trend' do not clarify to themselves whether they have actually selected the Marxian, or similar, constituents of the 'species essence' as values; they describe these simply as unalterable psychological facts. For instance Fromm, in *Man for Himself*, states as fact that the good is 'primary' whereas the bad is a 'secondary' potentiality in man. Then he adds: '. . . the development of the potentiality called 'primary' occurs under normal conditions', whereas the 'secondary' potentiality comes into manifest existence only in case of abnormal, pathogenic conditions.[86] The vicious circle caused by the 'concealed' selection of values becomes evident here. Our chosen values are the 'good

---

[85] Fromm dedicates an entire book to the analysis of Marx's concept of 'human essence', in which he draws near this concept to his own by psychologizing the Marxian concept in an unacceptable manner.

[86] E. Fromm, *Man for Himself*, New York: Rinehart and Co., 1947, p. 218.

ones', and the society which promotes these is the 'sane' society; on the other hand, all societies which do not promote these are, consequently, sick, pathological. Thus history so far, if we take Fromm for his word, is the history of pathology or, at least, includes the history of pathology.

> The sources of norm for ethical conduct are to be found in man's nature itself; . . . moral norms are based upon man's inherent qualities, and . . . their violation results in mental and emotional disintegration.[87]

Thus it isn't the moral objectivations — their creation and mastering — which carry moral values, nothing new, not-yet-extant can ever come about in the history of man; everything exists already since the formation of man and within human 'nature' as something psychologically given, and the sole task of the norms is to express that which already exists.

This line of thought is expressed most pregnantly by the most important representative of the 'third trend', Maslow in the following terms:

> Man demonstrates in his own nature a pressure toward fuller and fuller Being, more and more perfect actualization of his humanness in exactly the same naturalistic, scientific sense that an acorn may be said to be 'pressing toward' being an oak tree. . . the culture is sun and food and water: it is not the seed.[88]

I believe it should be clear, by now, why I have resorted to the term naturalism of the theory of the personality in discussing the 'third trend'. Maslow's simile of the oak illuminates better than all else the unavoidable naturalism of this concept. The inalienable 'seed' of human 'nature' is 'sown' in every society. The objectivational system, the totality of this society is merely the 'nourishment' of this seed. The oak may grow tall, may be thwarted in its growth or may perish, but may only develop in the direction of its own inherent substance. Let me reiterate: human nature may be built in *ad infinitum* (the oaks of Maslow may reach the sky), but cannot be built in just any odd way. If the soil or the sun are not appropriate to its nature, it will perish, along with the forest.

The metaphor of the tree and the forest indicates, at the same time, another hitch (albeit deriving from the first, to be sure) pertaining to the conception of the 'third trend'. Namely, that the individual is primary, whereas relationships between individuals are secondary, since that certain essence of the species 'dwells' in every individual. Love is a species-specific capacity of man, and it is love that brings about relationships between 'the trees of the forest', and it depends on the soil whether this relationship can

---

[87] *Id.*, 7.
[88] Abraham H. Maslow, *Toward a Psychology of Being,* Princeton: D. Van Nostrand, 1962, pp. 151-52.

be realized. That the specific nature of the relationship between persons is not only soil but also the shaper of those human potentials which have construed it, that love itself is but a part of humanized human relations in general – of all this Maslow and his school make no mention.

I do not mean to deny that Maslow has hit upon something new and significant in psychological anthropology in his description of the love-relationship he deems so central, as well as in the description of the reception of objectivations through experiences (which he calls 'peak experiences'). Here I can only refer to the distinction he makes between the so-called D-love and B-love.[89] D-love is 'deficiency-love', the expression and satisfaction of 'Deficit need'. This is 'the perennial impulse aimed at love', which is present in every individual of every society, and not only in the form of an 'inner substantial potentiality', but also in a 'realized conscious form'. There can be no society without D-love, or without the satisfaction of the need aimed at it. As for B-love, the 'love for being', it is love aimed at the being of the other, the climax of which is the *amor dei intellectualis* in the Spinozist and Goethean meaning of the term. B-love, as opposed to D-love, is idiosyncratic: in societies up to now only some have actually reached it. The objective for the future is the establishment of a society which would make it possible for everyone, as sun or soil, etc., to reach the level of B-love, to reach the level where B-love will become a need for society, hence for the state of 'unsatisfaction' in love to cease. At times Maslow broadens the distinction: he speaks of familiarization with D and with B, or D and B needs in general.

By this distinction Maslow has described essentially the same thing I had attempted to describe in my book on *Everyday Life*: the distinction between particularist person and individual. I too have analysed the particularist behaviour and the particularist needs as present in every culture and in every individual, whereas the category of individual has seemed to me to be, as well, 'idiosyncratic'. I too have discussed the distinction with a future in mind in which individual behaviour should become attainable by everybody.[90]

There is a basic philosophical distinction, however, between our two concepts which, in the last analysis, resides in our differing interpretations of the species essence. In my opinion – as formulated in the aforementioned book – there is no 'species essence', 'human nature', or 'substance' inherent in every individual. There are not 'two' beings concealed in man, an authentic and an inauthentic one, and the function of the objectivations is not to facilitate the development of the inauthentic or impede

---

[89] The whole of Maslow's complex of ideas will be analysed in my theory of personality.
[90] In my book *Everyday Life* I made no reference to Maslow, because I was not as yet familiar with his work.

the development of the authentic. In my opinion particularist or in-dividual personality structures are relationships, the relationship of man to the objectivations of his world and to his self; the forming of the in-dividual relationship is not the development of the 'inner essence', but this development is constituted in the active acquisition of objectivations, in the selection between their values, and their constant transformation. Without the complex – and distanced – internalization and transfor-mation of these objectivations there can be no individual. It is by means of this internalization and intention that the individual acquires the species essence, from the point of view of his personality. He cannot ever become identical with that essence, for man is not an oak, and society is not a forest of oaks. The 'idiosyncratic' nature of the individual cannot cease even if every person becomes an individual, because the 'species character' is carried by mankind, whereas the individual person carries only the consciousness of this 'species character', and the consciousness of his relation to it.

Nor do I share the consensus of the 'third trend', according to which the inauthentic and authentic persons are synonymous with the categories of 'sick' and 'sane'.[91] At the same time I must emphasize that this doctrine has become an organic part of their picture of the world. If the substance 'dwells' in us then only the person who represents substance can be 'healthy' (the realization of the potentials of the other individuals is under 'blockade'). Thus the 'self-actualizing' person actualizes the substance of the species itself, and self-actualization is health itself. The 'symptoms' of alienation appear as pathological symptoms. As András Angyal writes: 'In the neurotic orientation, the things and events of the world appear as isolated items or fragments.'[92], or, 'While in the confident orientation the person feels, thinks and speaks as he is and not as he is 'supposed' to be, the neurotic, having settled for appearances, acts for the sake of effect.'[93]

This connection between alienation and neurosis may also be reversed. In this case the 'healthy' individual is the personality which prevails over alienation, the personality that is not alienated.

I do not claim hereby that the naturalism of the theory of personality disregards the 'world'; after all, sick person and sick society are correlated. I merely claim that, since the 'sick world' plays the role of *milieu* in their case, they do not seek the actual possibilities for the cessation of the alienation of the personality in the world itself. Rather, they show the

---

[91] For my debate with this idea see my chapter 'Moral and normal', in *A moral szociológiája vagy a szociológia morálja* (The sociology of morality or the morality of sociology), Budapest: Gondolat, 1964.

[92] András Angyal, 'The Theory of Universal Ambiguity' in Lindsay-Hall, *Theories of Personality*, 297.

[93] *Ibid.*

possibility in man; and, of course, I also claim that this possibility is of decisive importance, from my own point of view, as I make clear in this treatise. They would build their theory around this fact, it becomes the basis of their view of the future. To be sure, they all speak of certain social prerequisites. One such social prequisite, according to Maslow, would be the satisfaction of the 'deficit need', 'safety' of life, and that the 'preservation of existence' should not constitute a daily problem. 'Safety is a *sine qua non* precondition for love, which is a precondition for self-actualization.'[94] writes Maslow. Yet he is convinced that self-actualization is easy, and does not understand the origin of the fact that (according to his own data) only 1% of mankind is self-actualizing. He considers 'peak experience' a decisive aspect of self-actualization: or, translated into the words of Lukács, the catharsis resulting from the enjoyment of art. Yet Maslow seems astonished that the 'after-effect' is so exceptional in the lives of those who take pleasure in art – or, to use the terminology of Lukács, the 'after', the actualization of the catharsis in life itself. If the 'species essence' resides in man, then it is indeed a mystery why the majority of mankind is not 'self-actualizing', why they do not get rid of their self-alienation, when this would be equivalent to the 'true', the 'healthy', the 'valuable' life? Why indeed? They already have enough to eat or drink, they need not fear that on the morrow they will have no shelter, the objects sufficient for their self-preservation are available – why don't they then start off 'towards the paradise in front of them' (the expression is borrowed from Maslow), why don't they establish, as healthy human beings that they are, the healthy society?

Actually, we have no right to be ironical towards the representatives of the 'third school'. For they have formulated something truly essential, something paradigmatic, if you like. Because, even if it is not true that the individual can abolish his alienation in an alienated world, it is true that at least he can strive for the abolishment of his alienated relation to the sane world, and without such a striving a future commensurate to man is indeed unimaginable. Thus they have answered the question which I have raised in my introduction, and which I consider the fundamental question of our times, to wit whether the changing of human beings constituting society, or of society 'producing' human beings is or is not a 'chicken and egg' problem – along the lines of a perspective commensurate to our values. According to them, the species essence is primary with regard to society, hence society can be changed in the direction of the 'species essence' insofar as human beings change themselves, actualize their own substance. And this is not merely possible but, to refer to Maslow once again, easy. But since I question their concept of 'species essence', I must

[94] Abraham H. Maslow, *op. cit.*, 162.

question, by the same token, their solution: for all of this does not seem 'so easy' to me.

The 'third trend's' theory of aggression is organically connected with their general theory. Thus the sole source of aggression is the frailty, 'shaky' character of our self-esteem. The person who, to use my own terminology, has not become a fully developed individual, who is not self-actualizing, may easily see his 'self-esteem' challenged. Thus, as Gert and Mills[+] have shown in their work *Character and Social Structure*, even the 'challenge to one's habits' may lead to the challenge of 'self-esteem'. The consequence of the blockade of self-esteem, according to Allport, is projection on the one hand, regression on the other (infantilism and rage). The frustrated individual seeks to 'reconquer' his lost self-esteem in aggression (White and Lippit). The person who does not self-actualize (writes Erikson) does not develop frustration tolerance, that is to say the less the person is self-actualizing, the less 'tolerant', and the more likely to interpret everything as 'directed against himself', as frustration. If someone cannot actualize his true potentials, he will gather resentment against all those he considers the cause of his failure. If he cannot evoke love in the person he loves, he will hate the one he loved for the sake of the preservation of his self-esteem: it is not I, it is he who is the cause of my failure. And I could continue with the examples analysed by the 'third trend'.

Thus we have arrived at the end of the analysis of the theories of aggression; for it is the 'third trend' that has formulated the only theory of aggression which I find convincing and true. I too believe that aggressive behaviour, and its frequence, is not the inevitable manifestation of some aggressive 'drive', nor is it the reaction response to particular and isolated frustrating stimuli, nor is it the consequence of the failure of psychological hygiene in infancy, nor does it necessarily stem from the existence of groups. Our impulses assume the form of rage aimed at the humiliation or destruction of other human beings because we are particularist persons, because we do not have self-confidence and self-esteem relying on ourselves, because we cannot actualize our potentials, and all this makes us suffer. We react with aggression to individual, isolated frustrations, and we consider them frustrations, because they affect our whole personality, because we conceive of them as an 'offense' against our personality. We react aggressively against members of other groups because we project the lack of our self-esteem onto the existence or members of this group, because we can 'rationalize' our own weakness, our own lack of success by their existence and their successes. The psychological hygiene of our infancy has a frustrating 'after-effect' only if it is an organic part of the blockade of the development of our personality.

The developed individual always has self-esteem, if you prefer, he has 'confidence' in himself. He can have confidence in himself because he actualizes himself. This does not mean, however, that the individual cannot have particularist motives, nor does it mean that he never reacts aggressively to offenses that affect his particularist self which is an in-eliminable entity. The difference is 'simply' that he does not rationalize this aggression later on, he does not ideologize it, does not project it, but recognizes it as a particularist act, and is thus capable of making good for it and, not infrequently, of never repeating it.

All this does not mean that there are no individualities in whom aggression itself has become a life principle. Since I have already discussed this in detail in my book *Everyday Life* I will sumarise briefly: these persons have either chosen evil, as Shakespeare's monsters, or have consciously opted for egoism as an ideology of life, as a guiding principle. There is no point in saying much about the former category, for they are exceptional. The latter, however, are altogether too typical in the bourgeois society centered on competition. In this connection I will merely refer to what I have said in the previous chapter. There is a very straightforward relationship between society set on competition and the 'quantum of aggression'; and not only because, as I have already mentioned, competition frustrates both the successful and the unsuccessful, even if not to an equal extent (the latter in his self-esteem, the former in the fear of loss of self-esteem), but also because this society constitutes the subsoil for the formation of the aggressive individual.

Of course, I do not consider the theory of aggression of the 'third trend' the only possible scientific explanation: but I have selected it. I have selected it because, on the one hand, it uncovers an empirically verifiable correlation and, on the other hand, because it corresponds to my values and the prospect I had selected, and can be organically built into the whole of my philosophy of history.

Yet my interpretation of 'human essence' differs considerably from the one proposed by the 'third trend'. This distinction is not without consequences as to the theory of aggression as well. Moreover, the distinction pertains to the issue which I deem decisive, the issue of mediation. The decisive issue, as far as I am concerned, is how today's mankind can be transformed into a mankind where the aggressive behaviour characteristic of particularism, its rationalizations, etc., are no longer general and typical.

The answer implied by the concepts propounded by 'the third trend' are clear and simple. Every man must become self-realizer (and this is also possible), every man must work out a strong and unshakable ego (and this is also possible), the self-esteem of every man must become unassailable (and this is also possible). But how? The means are identical with the possibility: by every man realizing himself, developing a strong ego, and an unshakable self-esteem. Baron Münchausen of the 'third trend' retrieves himself from the swamp by his own hair, and seeks and finds the solution to our problem along purely anthropological lines.

But this is precisely what I have referred to as naturalism of the theory of personality, and have evaluated as utopistic in practice. Not because the prospect itself (in my opinion) cannot be achieved theoretically, and not because the man of the future cannot, indeed, be extrapolated from the man of the present (the representatives of the 'third trend' are well aware of this), but rather because the means of realization they have formulated are not actually the means of realization, but simply one of their important albeit subordinate aspects. Thus I must once again raise the initial raise the question: can human nature indeed be built in *ad infinitum* from the aspect of behaviour? And does this infinite possibility exist in only one direction, as the representatives of the 'third trend' claim?

*The Questions*

> Whether in the course of the construction of a tank trap 10,000 Russian women perish interests me only to the extent of knowing whether the tank-trap has been completed for the sake of Germany. (Himmler)

> All these people have to be fed, housed and dealt with in such a manner that with the least investment imaginable they should achieve the greatest productivity imaginable. (Sauckel)

> The commander of the Janovsky camp, Obersturmbannführer Willhaus, for the sake of sport and in order to entertain his wife and daughter, systematically fired his automatic weapon at the prisoners working at their workplace from the windows of his service lodgings. Sometimes he handed the weapon over to his wife, who also fired. On one occasion Willhaus, to please his nine year-old daughter, gave orders for two four-year olds to be thrown up into the air, while he fired at them. His daughter was thrilled and shouted: 'Daddy, do it again!'. And he did it again.

All three quotations come from the reports of the Nürnberg trials. If we analyse them one by one, it becomes clear that only in the murderous 'game' of Obersturmbannführer Willhaus do or can purely anthropological and psychological aspects play a part. We may say about him that he undoubtedly wanted to restore his self-esteem when firing at children hurled into the air, as obsessed of power. But it is also unquestionable that it isn't simply a matter of anthropological and psychological considerations.

If we assume a meeting between Maslow and the surviving child of Obersturmbannführer Willhaus, in the course of which Maslow would explain to the 40-year old, that she must actualize herself, and then she will no longer be aggressive, we can approximately imagine the 'result' of the conversation. But it may be objected that monsters of the Willhaus type are the exception, and few children have received such an 'upbringing'. Yet we also know – and I believe it is unnecessary to cite examples – that although we are dealing with an extreme case, nevertheless it is to some extent a 'representative' case. More exceptional would be the child who is not raised in an environment where aggressions and 'sports' humiliating other human beings occur daily, or occur at all.

The more significant aspects, however, can be found in the first two quotes, for they lack any 'anthropological element'. We are dealing with instrumental aggression as a norm, and it is demanded clearly on the basis of the alienated ethics and politics of alienated history being constituted in antagonistic integrations and conflicts of interest. It was this norm, and the social and psychological 'heritage' of the 'prehistory' expressed in it that not only gave Willhaus a 'free hand' for his aggressive 'games', but made the 'use' of another human being as a mere instrument, the disregard of the other's existence, into a habit, and even a 'virtue'. Again it may be objected that the example is extreme. And again I can only reply that the destruction of 10,000 Russian women for the sake of the construction of a tank-trap is indeed extreme, yet the person who, in his habits, does not use other human beings as mere instruments would also be rather exceptional – and once again I need not cite examples. The use of human beings as mere instruments is still a habit nowadays, and instrumental aggression ideologizes this as virtue even today, or at least as a 'necessary evil'.

'Let us actualize ourselves,' 'let us become individualities,' 'let us develop in ourselves an unassailable self-confidence' – but how? Anthropology, as I mean to show briefly, cannot reply to the question of 'how' at all. Anthropology can do but one thing: it may outline, justify, or claim the anthropological possibility of a solution or a prospect. Better said, it may exclude the impossibility of it. It may say, man does not have innate species-specific drives, thus he does not have aggressive instincts either. Hence it is anthropologically not impossible (i.e. it is anthropologically possible) that a humanity should come about, of which aggression is not typically characteristic. It can assert that man responds to the 'stimuli' of the 'outside world' always with his whole personality: thus a humanity, the individuals of which may rationally distinguish between the demands, and the norms aimed at them, according to their value and function, and to which the individuals would respond neither with aggression nor with apathy, is not impossible (hence it is possible). It may assert: a mankind in which every individual disposes of a sufficiently shakable 'self-esteem' in order not to have to re-establish his self-esteem by means of aggression is theoretically possible. And finally it may assert, in order to transcend the problem of aggression, that from an anthropological point of view it is possible to imagine a mankind where the values of the species may be built in, and are actually built into, every individual.

I may assert this much, and I will assert this much, but no more. Not only the answer to the how, but also the answer to the general possibilities of the how would be the exploration of such possibilities as remain outside the realm of anthropology. For here we must answer questions regarding the structural transformation of the whole of society.

The fact that these problems remain outside the realm of anthropology does not mean, of course, that they may not relate to anthropology. Insofar as I assert that human essence is also embodied in the objectivations, even if mostly in an alienated form, if following Marx, I discover the objectivized human psyche in the means of production, if I assert that the essence of man develops and evolves precisely in its objectification, then it is precisely these objectivations that constitute the main topics of anthropology. Therefore, it is not the object of analysis that remains 'outside the realm of anthropology', but rather the approach to this object, the point of view and manner of analysis. Should we start out, with the approach of philosophical anthropology, from the system of objectivations in general the result will remain the same as what we have reached before: the definition of an abstract possibility, the rejection of an abstract 'impossibility'. I may add, as Marx had clearly done, that at the present level of development of the objectivations of the species it is possible for everyone to appropriate social wealth, that is, the abolishment of alienation; in other words, at the present level of the development of objectivations, in the first place at the present level of development of the forces of production, the elimination of alienation, and the 'self-actualization' of every individual is not impossible, is not excluded. But there still remains for us to answer the question: how do we go about actualizing our self? And the answer given to the 'how', in the works of Marx as well, transcend the realm of anthropology. The objectivations as well as the human actions that constitute them are heterogeneous with regard to anthropology: thus economic analysis, the specific analysis of social structures, the critique and recommendations regarding political action and the opportunities thereof. In these objectivations anthropology, apart from the theoretical formulation of abstract possibilities, can only fill the function of value guidance.

Since my present study, as I have stated from the start, is of an anthropological character, an analysis of the problems indicated above would exceed the framework of my line of thought. Let therefore one example suffice to indicate why the problem of the relationship of 'man' to 'his world' becomes indeed a 'chicken or egg' problem within anthropology itself; and how this problem can be transcended, albeit only on the level of a program for the time being, by an approach that goes beyond anthroplogy.

Let us recall the few remarks I have made in connection with the quotes taken from the records of the Nurenberg trials. Today's man is 'created' by a certain environment, by a world bent on competition because of the very nature of its economic and social structure, in a way varying from culture to culture, by a world in which the striving for minimal investment and maximum 'results' is part of the very essence of the 'functioning' of economy and society, by a world in which a group of men, once again as a consequence of the substance of its economic and social structure, constitutes a means for another group, by a world which is constituted in the clash of particularist interests, and in which 'instrumental aggression' provides the norm even if not always in its most extreme form.

The members of this same society should shape a world, a social structure, in which all this does not exist, in which society is the union of free men rather than the clash of particularist interests, which is not built on competition, in which every person is a self-goal for the others as well, in which everyone can become self-actualizing, etc. And this is undoubtedly the 'chicken and egg' question, if discussed in such anthropological generalities.

Marx said the problem has to be rendered more concrete to find a solution. Let us, therefore, attempt to make it concrete in a specific instance; and, for the sake of simplicity, in a matter affecting the theory of aggression.

Present society is founded on the division of labour. Moreover, both on social and technical division of labour, and there is an organic relationship between the two (albeit there is no room to analyse the relationship here). Persons placing themselves at various positions in the division of labour may develop their various potentials, the significance of which varies even from the aspect of self-actualization. The central activity of the position occupied in the social division of labour (work) is self-actualizing only for a negligible minority of persons. In general, social recognition is not 'awarded' to real achievement, and achievement itself is mostly quantified, the standard is uniform, and alienated to boot. Therefore, the source of 'self-esteem' is usually not to be found in man himself, in the human individual, but rather in what man owns: property and position. This, however, is pseudo-self-esteem which cannot procure security for man. For property is something that may be lost even if the personality remains unchanged, furthermore, it may become lost along with the development of personality. On the other hand, as we have seen, the person 'blocked' in his self-actualization, the person who finds his self-confidence outside of himself, shows affinity to aggression.

The division of labour, however, cannot cease within the foreseeable future. But does this signify that it is theoretically impossible to get around the chicken or the egg question?

I believe if we raise the question in this manner 'the chicken or the egg' problem no longer exists. Instead, we find a number of equally realistic alternatives. What are these alternatives?

One would be the preservation of existing conditions. In this framework, division of labour, the man created by the division of labour, man recreating the division of labour and his present relations, may be extrapolated into the future. Technology may change, the human capacities put to use may change, but the structure of man and of the world is formed only in the framework of 'otherness'. There is no need to comment upon this prospect.

The other alternative: the 'building-in' of human 'nature' in the direction of maximum manipulation. Then the social division of labour would not only remain, but may even increase. A technological 'elite' would 'build in' the 'nature' of the persons occupying the lower rungs of the division of labour in accordance with its own interests. This may become possible – though today it seems still utopistic – through the transformation of the genetic code (as many have already imagined), but perhaps even without such a transformation. Thus the tendency to build in would lead to the decrease of the need for self-actualization among the majority of individuals. And if self-actualization is no longer a need, 'self-esteem' would cease to be one as well. Aggression 'dies out', not because every person has become self-actualizing, but because the need for self-actualization has died out.

The representatives of the 'third trend', as we have seen, deny the reality of this prospect. They argue – as you may recall – that the need for self-actualization cannot be eliminated from man, hence its blocking would lead to psychological disturbances which in the long run would render society disfunctional. Perhaps this is not impossible, but I remain unconvinced, if only because the lessons of history certainly do not indicate that only the 'good' can be built into human 'nature'. In my opinion, the 'infinite' capacity to build in undoubtedly has a negative alternative.

The third opportunity – the one I have chosen – is not based upon the prospect of the immediate demolition of the division of labour. Two factors play a part in the shaping of this alternative. The first are the social and economic conditions for the transformation of the division of labour; the second, the existence of social forces that could become the 'carriers' of such a transformation.

To make proposals for the model of the new kind of division of labour would be, from the point of view of the problem under discussion, a task of critical economics and sociology. I just want to refer to certain issues to be solved. One would be the mechanization of the types of labour that do not provide self-actualization in any respect, the diminution of intensity in types of labour that have become dehumanized because of excessive intensity, the decrease in working hours required by society, the guarantee of the possibility of active decision-making by every individual in his own work area, the creation of the opportunity to acquire the know-how necessary for such participation, the cessation of the division of labour in all places where this division is justified not by vocational training but merely by the system of prestige of the social division of labour, and the opportunity for people to objectify their personality as well as their products. Even this slight, and altogether realistic departure from the predominant structure of the division of labour would make it possible for forms of self-actualization and self-esteem less oriented towards property to become more general, and would influence innumerable social relations that have little to do with the division of labour or are only distantly related to it.

What social forces may 'carry' these and similar trends? I believe we must differentiate between two basic types of such 'carrying media'. The first type would include those who suffer the most severely from the lack of opportunity for self-actualization, which again means two things: that their style of life and activity is not *de facto* self-actualizing, but their potentials and needs are such that they are conscious of it, that they feel the 'lack'. The second type would include those who are already *de facto* self-actualizing, or at least have the opportunity to become so, hence they challenge society geared towards the value of property inasmuch as they consider their own values and attitudes paradigmatic, generalizable, and to be generalized.

Undoubtedly, the direct possibilities sketched in this third alternative do not contain in themselves 'paradise standing in front of us' (the expression of Maslow). To start off and arrive somewhere simultaneously can only happen if we remain in place. More than one generation has already deluded itself with the promise of paradise in the immediate future. Whether they believed that standing in place is arriving, or whether they turned away disillusioned from an existence that was very distant from any sort of paradise, one thing was for certain: the promise of 'paradise' produced not less frustrated people as being abandoned to the acceptance of the specific nature of reality as such in a resigned manner. For what can be more frustrating in our self-esteem than the impossibility to realize the faith assumed in complete self-actualization? Yet it is also true: if we don't know where we want to arrive we cannot even start off, and it is our duty to examine at each and every moment whether we have indeed started off in the right direction.

I have given but one example, and an undoubtedly slimly documented one at that, for the three alternatives. But I believe we may confront any 'chicken-and-egg' problem presented by anthropology and, if we make it specific, we would reach the same three alternatives.

Man is not born with inalienable instincts, since he is not born with instinct at all. Nor is he a 'blank page' which may be conditioned by everything according to the spur of the moment. Nor is he, however, an embodiment of the innate essence of the species, of the human substance. Man does have a 'second nature'. This second nature has developed historically and finds incarnation in the objectivations, and in the individuals of the present world, as a matter of reciprocal influence. The concrete potentials contained in the present are part and parcel of this 'nature', both in the direction of the negative and of the positive alternatives. I claim that the 'building-in' of the 'species essence' into the 'second nature' is both possible and desirable; and this belief is derived not from my 'optimism', but from my choice. I do not mean to predict such a future, but to set questions to it.